CAN YOU TRUST THE BIBLE?

Jesus is The Way
Follow Him *all* the Way.

With love, — Hi

Frances Hogan

Can You Trust the Bible?
A Popular Guide for Catholics

Frances Hogan

Servant Publications
Ann Arbor, Michigan

Excerpts from Scripture are taken from the Jerusalem Bible,
copyright © 1966, 1967, and 1968 by Darton, Longman & Todd
Ltd. and Doubleday & Company, Inc. and are used by
permission of the copyright holder.

Scripture used in the Appendix is from the New International
Version of the Bible, copyright © 1978 by New York
International Bible Society, used by permission of Zondervan
Bible Publishers.

With Ecclesiastical Permission: Martin Hogan, L.S.S., Dublin,
Ireland, January 20, 1991.

Published by Servant Books
P.O. Box 8617
Ann Arbor, Michigan 48107

Cover design by Michael Andaloro
Cover photo by David Knox

91 92 93 94 10 9 8 7 6 5 4 3 2 1

Printed in the United States of America
ISBN 0-89283-694-6

Library of Congress Cataloging-in-Publication Data

Hogan, Frances, 1941-
    Can you trust the Bible? : a popular guide for Catholics /
Frances Hogan.
        p.   cm.
    ISBN 0-89283-694-6
    1. Bible—Evidences, authority, etc.   2. Bible—Hermeneutics.
3. Catholic Church—Doctrines.   I. Title.
BS480.H56   1991
220.6'1'02422—dc20   90-26092

Contents

Part VI: Ultimate Realities

Introduction

CHANGING AN ELECTRICAL PLUG on a household gadget is a far cry from the experiments carried out in university laboratories. Many people who claim no interest in scientific research are nonetheless happy to apply its results in the safe use of electrical power in the home. Two very important things are touched upon here that are pertinent to this book. First, we need experts working on their scientific investigations in order to have progress. Second, practical applications of the fruits of scientific investigation can yield a safer, more comfortable, more efficient lifestyle.

Too little knowledge is a dangerous thing. This is true of electricity in the home; it is certainly true of the Scriptures. Many of us are uncomfortable with the Bible because of all that trickles down to us from the esoteric heights of biblical scholars. Fundamentalists claim absolute certainty on everything. Liberals question everything, even the historicity of the Gospels. Scientists have questioned the authenticity of the Creation accounts in Genesis. Archeologists have added fuel to the fire by claiming to disprove some of the dating in the Old Testament. In all this confusion, how could anyone really trust the Bible anymore?

In the midst of all this confusion, we Christians know that the Bible is the written Word of God. In this book I would like to deepen in us an awareness of that truth. Yes, I hope to answer the critics, but more than that, to share with you the awe I experience as I read and study the Bible. We can grow in our love for the Lord as we research the words of men looking for the Word of God. The more we study the Bible, the more fascinating the research becomes, and the more one marvels at the ways of God in dealing with his beloved children.

Each generation challenges the Bible in some way. This challenge is an opportunity to seek the Lord for guidance. The generations before us found the answers to their questions, and so will we.

Our generation is questioning the historicity of the Gospel accounts. Watch how the Lord will provide proof after proof to help those who are sincerely seeking the truth. (No amount of proof will help those who do not want to be persuaded.) I will show in the sections on manuscripts and archeology just how kind the Lord has been in furnishing proofs.

We should not be disturbed by the controversies over the Bible, nor by the interim explanations given by scholars en route to deeper knowledge. All this research is necessary and good, but like electricity, the information needs to be handled in such a way that it will give life, not snuff it out! I believe that we have reached a mature stage with regard to the Scriptures and with regard to our Christian faith as a result of all that is going on. None of us can get by anymore on an uneducated or uninformed faith.

Just as we have progressed dramatically in science and technology in this century, so now we hope to progress with regard to the sacred sciences, namely, the knowledge of the Scriptures and the knowledge of God. As we explore outer space, so we need to explore "inner space," the tabernacle of God on earth that is our own beings. Our reasons for believing must be based on facts, not on "we always did it this way." Where Scripture is concerned, most of us are overdue for a refresher course. I hope you enjoy this book as an introduction to such a course.

This book is not written by an expert for experts, but by a believer for believers. I assume that the reader accepts the authority of the church to teach and guide us in matters of faith and morals. I also assume that you accept the two sources of revelation, namely Tradition and Scripture. This book will attempt to show you that they cannot be separated without distortion, for the church today is the same reality as the church of the Apostles, and a continuation of it. Now the vine has twentieth-century branches instead of first-century ones, and it has accumulated much knowledge and experience in the intervening period. This increased knowledge increases our responsibility to obey the Word and to proclaim it.

This book contains four parts. The first three treat general matters pertaining to both the Old Testament and the New Testament: their origins, their authenticity, and the search for their meaning. Each topic is illustrated with examples, so that you are not faced with pure theory. I am not attempting a full treatise on any of the subjects touched upon. If an explanation is still at the theory stage, that is stated clearly. I hope that the few examples given will stimulate a desire for more study on the subject, and thus open up for you the wonders of the biblical world.

The fourth section deals exclusively with the New Testament, which has been the subject of extensive research for the past hundred years. Among scholars of the New Testament there is such divergence of opinion that many ordinary people have lost confidence in its authenticity. Some scholars question the very foundations of our faith. I stand firmly by Tradition, the early church fathers, and the church's magisterium today.

It is not the prerogative of scholars to give us a new faith, rather they are to illumine the old one. It is their privilege to explain the Scriptures, not to destroy them. The Holy Spirit is our illuminator, the One to whom both scholar and believer must turn.

Part I

The Problem of Origins

ONE

A Book with a History

I TS MOST RECENT SECTIONS are two thousand years old, and yet the Bible remains the world's number-one bestseller. It is the best preserved of all the ancient texts. Translated into numerous languages, it is used by people on every continent on earth. People have died for the privilege of reading the Bible; others have risked their lives to bring it into countries where it was banned.

The Bible has influenced the whole history of civilization. From its laws have developed legal codes found in many middle eastern and western civilizations. Its main theme is the history of salvation, in which we all have a part. Because this history is imbedded in the history of Israel, no civilization is more studied and better known than that of the Middle East. Today millions of people read the Bible on a daily basis, looking for life and direction just as their forebearers did in previous centuries. Yes, even the modern world with all its sophistication needs the spiritual nourishment that comes from reading God's Word.

Yet many ordinary people today are upset by what they have heard from the scholars, the skeptics, the scientists. They hear questions being raised concerning the veracity of what the Bible teaches. Since they do not have the opportunity or the learning to check these things for themselves, they are tempted to put the Bible aside for fear of being led astray. This is a great pity, for we cannot afford to be without the treasure of God's Word.

GOD'S WORD ON SCROLLS AND SKINS

The Bible is one of the best preserved of all known manuscript traditions. Indeed, many of the masterpieces of ancient Greco-Roman literature have only a few manuscripts preserved—less than a dozen in the case of the works of Julius Caesar, for example, and they date from the ninth and tenth century.

The Shrine of the Book in Jerusalem houses the oldest text of Isaiah, approximately 2,200 years old. If you compare the 3rd century, B.C. Isaiah scroll with the 10th century, A.D. Hebrew text of Isaiah prepared by the Masorettes, you will see a very high degree of agreement in almost every single instance. Thousands of scribes through two and a half millennia have considered God's Word so sacred that they were determined to copy it exactly.

The ancient world did not have books as we know them. Ancient scholars wrote on papyrus, a type of paper made from the plentiful papyrus reed plant. The Egyptians, Greeks, and Romans glued the sheets of papyrus together to make long scrolls. One can see how difficult it would be to preserve these scrolls, yet hundreds of fragments are extant, and they are invaluable to scholars.

The alternative to papyrus was to use stretched animal skins. The skins were stitched together to make scrolls. The Isaiah scroll mentioned earlier is written on seventeen strips of animal skins stitched together to make a scroll twenty-four and one-half feet long and ten and one-half inches high. The text is written in columns.

The twentieth century has been an era of exciting discoveries of biblical manuscripts. The greatest of these was the Dead Sea Scrolls. They are the remains of a whole library, and were found by accident in 1947 by a Bedouin shepherd. The discovery was made beside the ruins of the monastery at Qumran, where monks of a Jewish sect, called the Essenes, had lived.

The Shrine of the Book in Jerusalem displays many of the finds from the four caves at Qumran. Among them are fragments of six hundred manuscripts from all of the Old Testament except the Book of Esther. The most important manuscript found is the complete scroll of Isaiah. All of these manuscripts are one thousand years older than the oldest copy in use before this discovery. Other archeological finds around Judea have yielded nearly two hundred other Old Testament manuscripts, including those found at the fortress of Masada, site of an ancient Jewish settlement.

Before these discoveries the oldest complete Old Testament text was called the Masoretic text, which comes from the meticulous work of scribes from the sixth to the tenth century A.D. The amazing fact is that the manuscripts from the first century B.C. are the same as the Masoretic text, testifying to the fidelity of the scribes in transmitting the Word of God down through the centuries.

A LONG HISTORY: 2000 B.C.-A.D. 2000

Each book of the Old Testament has a long history of development. Every synagogue had its own complete set of scrolls, so many manuscripts were in use, each one copied from a previous one. A book "grew" over a period of time, as scribes understood more of the implications of the text, and added explanatory notes or comments. Thus small variations have been found in some manuscripts. These enable scholars to interpret the mind of the people at the time of writing and to understand what they meant by certain phrases.

By the first century A.D., after the fall of Jerusalem, a group of Jewish scholars came together to finalize a text from the manuscripts that had survived the burning of the temple in A.D. 70. They deleted any additions or explanations, just leaving the naked text. The Isaian scroll of Qumran is the same as the so-called final text, testifying to the fact that the final form of the Old Testament came into being before or during the time of Christ. These texts agree with the Masoretic text also, which is the official Jewish text even to this day.

The Masoretic text derives its name from the Hebrew *masoret* which means "tradition." The rabbis who worked meticulously to keep this tradition of the Word of God intact were called the Masorettes. From their scholarly work on manuscripts and fragments of the Hebrew text between the sixth and tenth centuries came the certainty of the Old Testament text. They adhered to stringent rules in transmitting the text and removed any additions, thus preserving the text from further variation.

The original Hebrew manuscripts were written without the vowel signs. The pronunciation of the text was passed on by word of mouth. The Masorettes put the vowel signs into the text so that future generations could read it directly. This amounted to putting in dots or points above or below the words to help in pronunciation. They also put indications in the margins to help with difficult or rare words and phrases. All new copies of this text kept the vowel signs and marginal extras, and it is this final Hebrew text that is called the Old Testament by Christians. One can see that the text of the Old Testament is the work not only of the original authors, but also of the community of believers.

As the Jewish community moved into the Hellenistic world, and Hebrew began to fall into disuse, a need arose for Aramaic translations of the Hebrew texts. These are called Targums. The word *Targum* means "version." The sacred Hebrew text was retained for public worship, but the Targums were necessary for everyday usage. A set of these important translations is in the Vatican library.

The Septuagint is a Greek translation of the Hebrew Old Testament dating back to the second century B.C. According to ancient tradition, it is the work of seventy-two scholars of Alexandria, in Egypt—hence the name. This translation includes the original texts of the later books of the Old Testament, called by some the deuterocanonical books. They are 1 and 2 Maccabees, Wisdom, Tobit, Judith, Baruch, Sirach, and parts of Esther and Daniel. Some of these texts were originally written in Hebrew, but all have survived in Greek because of the dominance of Greek culture at that time. It was this version of the Old Testament that was most used by the early church as it spread throughout Greece and Asia Minor. It is still the dominant text used by millions of Christians in the Eastern Orthodox church.

Apart from these texts there is the Samaritan Pentateuch and many manuscripts in other languages, as the Scriptures were used all over the Middle East. When modern scholars work on a new translation of the Bible they pore over hundreds of these manuscripts in order to render every word as accurately as possible.

THE NEW TESTAMENT

In the New Testament manuscripts we have an embarrassment of riches. The New Testament was written in Greek in the first century of the Christian era. It was produced in codex, or book form. The oldest copies (codices) available until the nineteenth century, were from A.D. 350. Recent discoveries have uncovered earlier texts. For example, the John Rylands Library in Manchester, England, has parts of John's Gospel from A.D. 130, about forty years after the Gospel was finalized. The Chester Beatty Library in Dublin has parts of the Gospels, Acts, and the letters of Paul dating from A.D. 200 to 300. The Bodmer Library in Geneva has fourteen chapters of John's Gospel and other New Testament material from about A.D. 200. As with the Old Testament, the Gospels, Acts, Epistles, and Revelation had to be copied by hand, and every church group needed a full set.

Like the books of the Old Testament, the material found in the books of the New Testament "grew" during the early days of the church, until they were collected and fixed in their final written form. The New Testament, therefore, like the Old, is the work of the original authors within the context of the Church, the community of believers, who added explanation and insight to the text before its final form. The sacred authors of both the Old Testament and the New Testament worked under the inspiration of the Holy Spirit to give us this wonderful testimony to the work of God. Their work exemplifies Jesus' clear teaching that the Holy Spirit will remain with us *forever* and that he will be our teacher throughout the time of the church (see Jn 14:16, 26; 16:12-14).

The discoveries of the twentieth century have uncovered many important papyri and codices of the New Testament. So great are these discoveries that we who live almost two thousand years after Christ have more accurate renderings of his teaching in our modern Bibles than was available to our ancestors. Present-day scholars have such an abundance of material to work with that they are more sure now than ever before of the accuracy of the text. While many people cling to older translations as more familiar, the more recent translations of the Bible incorporate the findings of scholars and are therefore more reliable as translations.

An amazing fact is that when scholars examine the many important papyri discovered recently, they find no reading of the text that would change any essential Christian teaching. Fidelity in copying the New Testament has been remarkable, especially when one considers the numerous hands at work all over Europe, the Middle East, and North

Africa. Truly the Lord took care of his Word, as he promised the prophet Jeremiah he would do (see Jer 1:11-12).

ENGLISH BIBLES

Within a century of the conversion of England by Augustine in A.D. 600, Anglo-Saxon translations of the Bible began to appear. After the Norman conquest, Anglo-Norman translations were produced. These were used into the Middle Ages, when the Wycliffe movement produced parts of the Bible in English. The first complete translation of the Bible into English is thus associated with John Wycliffe and dated 1384. This became the popular Bible of fifteenth- and sixteenth-century England. It was based on the earlier official Vulgate version in common use in the church.

The Protestant Reformation in England produced other Bibles, notably the Tyndale Bible of 1530. This had virulent anti-Catholic notes and strong theological bias, but its English was good. Coverdale's Bible in 1535 was a less reliable version based on secondary sources. It was followed by the Great Bible of 1541, which became the first official Bible in the vernacular and was used in every church in England. Its translator, John Rogers, relied both on Tyndale and on Coverdale, as well as the Latin Vulgate. Its Psalter was used in *The Book of Common Prayer*.

The Geneva Bible was produced in 1558 by English Protestants in exile during the reign of the Catholic Queen Mary I. It improved Tyndale and the Great Bible, and was used for private reading by many at the time. It greatly influenced Shakespeare, the Puritans, and Bunyan, for example. The Bishop's Bible in 1568 was a revision of the Great Bible in the light of the Geneva Bible. Then came the most influential translation in English until modern times, the King James Version. Work began on the King James Version in 1604. This Bible became known as the Authorized

Version. It remained popular up to recent times. This Bible was an improvement on the Bishop's Bible and other earlier versions. In 1881 scholars began work on a revised King James Version. This was followed by the American Standard Version in 1901.

The next major translation was the Revised Standard Version, which appeared in 1952. Here new scholarship was available to the translators, but the text remained faithful to the older translations unless it was absolutely necessary to change it. The Catholic edition, containing the deutero-canonical books, appeared in 1966.

Since this time, with the stimulus of new scholarship and also the desire to provide Bibles in today's English, there have been numerous other translations. The more widely used are the New English Bible of 1970 and Today's English Version, also called the Good News Bible, brought out in 1979. The New International Version of 1978 was produced by teams of scholars from thirty-four different religious groups working in twenty teams, incorporating the latest discoveries and scholarship.

Specifically Catholic versions of the Bible became an issue after the Reformation. The Council of Trent insisted on the Latin Vulgate translation as the official one for the church. The Vulgate is Jerome's Latin translation of the whole Bible from the original Hebrew and Greek texts available to him. Latin was used by the whole church at that time. Jerome began his work of translation in about 389. So the Vulgate is the oldest official translation used by the church and a wonderful testimony to the work of scholarship that left us with a coherent Bible.

The Douay-Rheims version of 1609 was produced by Catholic English scholars in exile on the continent of Europe. It was good, even if it contained Latinisms that later scholars would not accept. This translation influenced the Author-ized Version also. The Challoner revision of the Douay-Rheims came out in 1763. This remained the Bible of English-speaking Catholics for two hundred years. Then came the Confraternity revision of the New Testament in 1941 and the Knox Bible in 1950.

When Pope Pius XII permitted work on new translations using the original manuscripts, completely new translations appeared. The most notable of these were the New American Bible in 1970 and its revised New Testament in 1985 (which come with an Imprimatur) and the Jerusalem Bible in 1966 and 1985.

As more discoveries are made, we can expect scholars to develop ever more accurate translations. We can be grateful to scholars who work for long years on obscure manuscripts. They make an accurate rendering of God's holy Word available to those who could not read the original documents for themselves.

TWO

Who Wrote the Bible?

FOR THE UNINITIATED, THIS QUESTION READS LIKE, "Who wrote Handel's Messiah?"

The answer appears obvious: Matthew wrote Matthew's Gospel; Paul wrote Paul's letters; John wrote Revelation, and so on. But is it that simple?

Did Moses write the Pentateuch, for example? If he did, then he had the unique privilege of describing his own death, funeral, and subsequent fame in Deuteronomy 34! Nor is it possible that David, who lived 1,000 years before Christ, wrote all the Psalms. Psalm 126, for example, was written after the Exile, which took place in 587 B.C. (nearly 500 years later). The Book of Psalms as we have it today is the result of more than eight hundred years of liturgical life and literary activity in Israel. David is the most famous psalmist, and therefore the one to whom the entire collection is dedicated.

Let us state for the sake of clarity that the Holy Spirit is the most important author of the Bible. In his divine wisdom he knew whom to choose to write God's Word and how to inspire those chosen. He also knew how to watch over his Word, as he whispered to Jeremiah (Jer 1:12). The Spirit of God watched over the whole formation of the Bible at every stage of its development, as it passed through hundreds of scribes, translators, and editors down through the centuries. He ensured that God's revelation would come to us intact.

Nevertheless, the Bible bears the marks of human transmission. It is a document that, like Jesus, its main subject, is both human and divine, and it bears the marks of both of its origins (Heb 4:12). Later in this book I will look at the divine author. Here we examine the human authors who cooperated with this divine hand in the transmission of God's Word.

MOSES' FIVE BOOKS

The Hebrew Bible calls this work the Torah, or the written law, and it is the most cherished part of the Old Testament Scriptures. Since it consists of five distinct parts—namely Genesis (the Beginnings), Exodus (the Going Out), Leviticus (from Levi, the priestly tribe), Numbers (which concerns the wilderness but speaks of the census in the first few chapters), and finally Deuteronomy (which means the revision of the law or the second law)—the Greeks and Hellenistic Jews called it the Pentateuch, or the five-part work.

The authorship of the Pentateuch is not only a scholarly problem. It impinges on the faith of all believers, for Moses was God's chief lawgiver before the coming of Jesus. He gave us what we call the natural law, on which society is based. It is therefore imperative to find out who or what authority lies behind the great work that is attributed to Moses.

That Moses is the authority behind the Pentateuch cannot be reasonably doubted. Exodus 24:4 says, for example, that Moses put all the commands of the Lord into writing (see also Ex 34:27; Dt 31:9). But in what sense is he the author? His position as the teaching authority behind the Pentateuch is surely more important than that of the scribe who penned the material. The immense biblical research of the past century has shown the text of the Pentateuch to be so complex that it could not have originated from one scribe. Rather it appears to have come from several schools of theology, dealing with their subjects from different points of view.

MANY HANDS AT WORK

A reading of the Pentateuch leaves one feeling uneasy, for some events are given in duplicate with no attempt at reconciliation. There are two creation accounts, in Genesis 1 and Genesis 2; two accounts of the covenant with Abraham, in Genesis 15 and Genesis 17; two dismissals of Hagar, in Genesis 16 and Genesis 21; two accounts of Moses' call, in Exodus 3 and Exodus 6; two water miracles at Meribah, in Exodus 17 and Numbers 20; and two texts of the Decalogue, in Exodus 20 and Deuteronomy 5.

There are also two cases of Abraham passing his wife off as his sister: Genesis 12:10-20 in Egypt, and Genesis 20 in Gerar. An identical story is told of Isaac in Gerar in Genesis 26:6-11. The gifts of manna and quail are explained in Exodus 16 and Numbers 11. The naming of Bethel is given twice, in Genesis 28:19 and in Genesis 35:15. Some narratives like that of the Flood have repetitions and discordant statements that point to two divergent accounts (see Gn 6-8).

We can deal with the problem in several ways. One is the fundamentalist approach, which is to go to great lengths to reconcile both versions of a story. The other, preferred by Catholic scholars, is to admit that we are dealing with two versions and acknowledge different authorship for both accounts. A third tendency is to say that the Bible is all myth, stories to be told to children but not taken seriously by adults. Others even throw away the Bible, saying that it is full of contradictions and errors.

Genesis begins with the first glaring example of duplication, the story of Creation. Genesis 1 presents the creation of the earth as a liturgical reading—that is, a text for use in public worship. The authors (who appear to be the priests of the temple in Jerusalem) present God as doing a certain amount of work each day. Then, like a good Israelite, he rests on the Sabbath! The presentation of the material is somewhat artificial, specially chosen by the authors to present the holiness of the Sabbath and to highlight the fact that God is the author of everything around us. One must not worship the sun, moon, or stars, for they are only creatures of the great Creator of the universe.

The authors are not teaching science; therefore their text should not be read as a scientific manual. Yet they tell us that God created inanimate matter first, before proceeding with the creation of plants, animals, and finally the human race. The authors seem to know that life on earth is impossible without light, which they put on the first day, and water, which they place on the second day.

Genesis 2 could not have come from either the same hands or the same school of theology as Genesis 1. Genesis 1 speaks of God in a distant, transcendent way, while chapters 2 and 3 speak of the Lord who is near us and involved with us. He creates us with great care. He is described as the great parent who is anxious to make his children happy in a lovely home on earth with everything they need. He gives them not only human life but spiritual life when he breathes the breath of God into them. But they must prove themselves worthy of the gift in a test of obedience. They can only continue as sons and daughters of God if they choose God's way, symbolized by the tree of life. Since they choose the tree of the knowledge of good and evil, they put themselves under the influence of the evil one. They also bring on themselves the consequences of evil—namely sickness and death.

Thus in story form these authors tell us about the Creation and the Fall in a way that is intelligible even to children. They also present the holiness of marriage and its origin in God. They highlight the special place of human beings above the rest of creation. In this text we can hear the ancient storyteller passing on the teaching of the ages to the next generation.

Since both Creation accounts are valuable in what they teach, the compilers of Genesis decided to leave them side by side. They realized that the two accounts make different points with regard to Creation and the Fall.

We can see from this example that we must not think of human biblical authorship in the modern sense, of a single hand producing a whole text. Authorship includes the person who gave the teaching in the first place, the teachers and preachers who passed it on, and those who compiled and edited the book in its final form. Thus the substance of the Pentateuch is Mosaic, but the text has passed through many hands before reaching the form in which we have it today.

For ancient peoples the message was more important than the scribe who committed it to paper. The name given to a book indicated whose teaching was being given. The people knew that the Pentateuch was the teaching of their great leader and lawgiver, Moses, and they treasured it.

THREE

The Four Old Testament Traditions

T HE PAST WOULD BE LOST FOREVER but for the fact that every civilization has handed on its tradition, beliefs, and history to successive generations by word of mouth. This process goes on continually in the home, in places of worship, and in both local and national groups within society. This oral tradition has been the most important educational tool in every civilization. Even in modern times it is the way most of us learn about hygiene, about local traditions, and about our faith. In ages preceding books, oral tradition was much more important than it is today in western society. Between the age of the patriarchs and the writing of their history is a lapse of eight hundred years; between Moses and the writing of the Levitical precepts there is a span of about seven hundred years. Oral tradition fills the gap.

The teaching of Moses was written down and preserved in the different major shrines of Israel. As this teaching was passed on to each successive generation, new insights were added. Each area had its own traditional ways of thinking about God and of passing on revelation about him. As a result of this process, four different traditions seem to be at work in the formation of the Pentateuch. They are called the Yahwist tradition (designated by the letter J), the Elohist tradition (E), the Deuteronomist tradition (D), and finally the Priestly tradition (P). This "classic documentary theory," as scholars refer to it, appears to be the best way to explain the differences in composition, style, and theology, as well as the various repetitions and apparent contradictions in the text of the Pentateuch. As more discoveries are made, either a refinement of this theory or a replacement by a better explanation will emerge.

The age of the texts is important. The original Mosaic material goes back to the thirteenth century before Christ. Few people in those days would have been able to read or write, so the teaching had to be given by the preachers and teachers. In an age where no written visual aids were possible, the teaching was encapsuled in sagas, poems, songs, and dramas in order to bring it alive for the listeners. Hence the storytellers, the bards, and the minstrels would have played an important part in the transmission of the material.

On the other hand, the legal code, which was given to the priests to govern the people, would have been studied and developed as need arose. The people would have heard this teaching in different ways. The priests were interested in formal readings for public worship, where the teaching was presented crisply and clearly.

THE STORYTELLER'S VERSION

The Yahwist or J document is said to have been finalized in the tenth century B.C., two hundred to three hundred years after Moses' time. It is characterized by the way it uses the name Yahweh; or Lord, for God. The E and P traditions claim that this name was revealed later to Moses (Ex 3:13-15; 6:2-3). Therefore any account that uses the name Yahweh in telling events prior to Moses comes from the J tradition.

The J document speaks of the Lord being very close to us and involved with us. Its story form makes for easy reading. It is to the Yahwist group that we owe such lovely images of God as the One who walks with Adam in the cool of the day, who made clothes for Adam and Eve (Gn 3), who talks to Cain in order to help him avoid temptation, and who does not reject the sinner even when the sinner rejects him (Gn 4). This document speaks of God in a very human way, even letting us see God's regret at having made humans when the earth becomes polluted by sin (Gn 6:5-7). The value of this type of teaching is that the audience can see things from God's point of view and hopefully come to repent more easily.

The J source provides the outline for much of the content of the first four books of the Pentateuch. The E source deals with the same material as the J but in a different style— hence the repetitions. Together, these sources testify to the fact that oral traditions were kept alive in both kingdoms, north and south of Israel. Both traditions go back to Moses.

The style of the J document is so distinctive that it would appear to be the work of one individual. He has been described as a religious genius and one of the world's greatest literary figures. His stories have been imprinted on the minds and hearts of the greater part of western civilization for three millennia. He comes from the tenth century B.C., the time of Israel's greatest glory under David and Solomon, and this obviously influenced his thinking. This age was known to have been one of great religious reform and liturgical activity.

The Yahwist author proclaims that it is possible for humans to have a genuine intimacy with God. Sin is the breaking of that intimacy, the ultimate tragedy, and the source of all our woes. He says that this world is a paradise or a hell depending on whether we live according to the will of him who made us in love. The Yahwist shows how sin affects society. Yet with equal sensitivity he reveals the loving-kindness of God, his willingness to forgive and redeem. The events of history are not given in dry doctrinal statements but in the "blood 'n guts" of everyday life, where real characters are revealed through their thoughts and words. The Yahwist is like a preacher who seeks involvement from his audience. He wants a response of repentance, much as Jesus did in his wonderful story of the prodigal son.

The ancient Yahwist source tells us that Cain and Abel, as well as Noah, offered sacrifice to God in a past which was distant even for him. Thus he shows that God has had his witnesses in every age. Although J speaks of God in very human terms, his image of God is exalted and pure. He portrays him as the Lord of Creation and of history, whose divine will governs the universe. As God used Moses as liberator and lawgiver, he also used the Yahwist author to reveal the Word of God to us.

CONFRONTING AN AWESOME GOD

The Yahwist tradition of teaching persisted until the breakup of Israel into two distinct kingdoms. A new way of conveying the same basic teaching developed in the prophetic circles of the northern kingdom in the ninth century B.C. By the eighth century the new Elohist (E) document was a reality.

This document speaks of God in a distant, transcendent, almost abstract manner. God reveals himself through dreams or by means of an angel (Gn 20:3; 31:10-13; 46:2). Like J, E stresses God's providence in guiding his people. The Elohist's most famous text is the testing of Abraham in Genesis 22. Because the northern kingdom had a hard struggle against pagan influences, E scrupulously avoids ascribing to God any human characteristics, and insists on the prohibition against sculptured images of the Godhead (Ex 20:4).

Whereas J shows apparitions of God as friendly and intimate, E portrays them as mysterious, remote, and foreboding. God is referred to as *Elohim,* or God the Supreme One. He creates the world by his word alone. The style of this document is dry and terse, lacking the emotional appeal of J. Nevertheless, its theological insights were so valuable that John the evangelist used them to explain the Word becoming flesh in the Incarnation.

After the fall of the northern kingdom in 722 B.C., the E document was brought south to Jerusalem and fused with the J text. Most of Numbers consists of this combined text.

EXHORTATIONS TO HOLINESS

The Deuteronomist (D) tradition is found almost exclusively in the book of Deuteronomy. This book is the link between the Pentateuch and the historical books of Joshua, Judges, 1 and 2 Samuel, and 1 and 2 Kings, which it influenced greatly. The book of Jeremiah also contains D influence, which is not surprising, as it was Jeremiah and King Josiah who led the Deuteronomic reform. This reform had a profound effect on the thinking of Israel as a people. More than any other tradition, the Deuteronomist prepared the way for Christian revelation. When citing the Scriptures Jesus often quoted Deuteronomy (see, for example, Dt 6:4; Mt 22:37).

What distinguishes D from the other traditions is the emphasis on the personal relationship between the Lord and his people. He is the Lord, our God, who is full of compassion and love for his chosen people. God's love and the Exodus are the two favorite themes of D. God's love demands love in return, so God's service can never be lip service: it must always be from the heart (Dt 6). Unless external ritual finds expression in a genuine spiritual life, D does not accept it as real religion.

Deuteronomy is a profound and beautiful book. Its invitation to love God with our whole heart, soul, mind, and being is as attractive and demanding to our twentieth century as it was to any other age. On the level of national reform, D wants one God served in one temple by one nation. Can we not see this same plea in Jesus' prayer for the unity of God's people (Jn 17)?

Deuteronomy can be called a sustained exhortation to faithfulness to the Covenant and loyal obedience to the law. The whole book is presented as coming from the mouth of Moses. In 622 B.C. the "Book of the Law" was discovered in the temple during King Josiah's reform. This book is assumed to be either all or part of Deuteronomy (2 Kgs 22-23). The book disturbed the king, especially when he read the curses for those who did not observe the law (Dt 28). The subsequent reform that he carried out was done in accordance with the instructions of Deuteronomy.

It seems that Deuteronomy came from the northern kingdom, as some of its reference material is similar to the E tradition—using the name Horeb for Sinai, for instance. Many of its laws come from the Covenant code represented by the E document also. It seems that this book represents the preaching of the Levites, given in the northern shrines during ceremonies of renewal of the Covenant. After the fall of Samaria, some priests and Levites fled to the south to escape being exiled. The sacred scrolls they brought with them became additional source material for the compilers and editors of the Pentateuch.

LEGAL FOUNDATIONS

This was the last tradition to develop. It was the work of priests in Jerusalem, based on sources going back to Moses. The P tradition became very strong after the Exile in 538 B.C. This was the time of the restoration of the temple, and the priests had to formulate their religion very clearly for the returned exiles. It is no surprise, therefore, that the P document is concerned with legal codes and is found almost exclusively in the book of Leviticus. It concerns mostly the laws governing the practice of religion, and it demands that its rituals be followed to the letter. This rigidity was necessary at that time to correct abuses, but it gave rise to the legalism that Jesus would later condemn.

This document is fond of genealogies, for the aristocratic and priestly families used their lineage to justify their roles in Israel. The Priestly tradition established the priests as the spiritual leaders of the people, a position held by the prophets before the Exile. It also restored Israel's unique rituals and way of life. We see the P influence continue in the Books of 1 and 2 Chronicles, Ezra, and Nehemiah.

The style of P is usually precise and monotonous. Examples are the first Creation account and the description of the tabernacle and its furnishings in Exodus 35 to 40. P's conception of God is exalted and transcendent. God accomplishes things by his word alone, needing neither vision nor dream as a vehicle of communication. The priests seek to form a holy people worthy of a holy God. They demand pure faith, one not based on signs. Other matters fade into the background. The Book of Leviticus is almost entirely of the P tradition. Some P passages are also found in Genesis, Exodus, and Numbers. They can be detected easily by the fact that the text is usually very abstract, with a marked preference for numbers, measurements, and repetitions. These passages may not make easy reading, but they are full of the love of God and have a deep sense of the sacred.

THE ONE PENTATEUCH

At some point in the sixth or fifth century B.C., some priests or scribes, the only people who had access to the sacred scrolls, fused the four documents together to make the Pentateuch. The type of editing they used was very different from that we use today, for when they found more than one version of a story, they kept both side by side. Thus they testified to the work of the Holy Spirit in the different parts of their land.

This documentary theory explains the repetitions and apparent contradictions in the Flood story, for example. We can now detect two Flood stories, coming from the J and P traditions and woven together. Some expected variations are found, such as in the number of animals, the source of the water, and the length of the Flood. The J elements are easily picked out, for they show that God is upset, that his heart grieves like that of a parent. He personally shuts the door of the ark. The essence of the two stories is the same: God punished the ancient world for its immorality, as he did not want the very fountains of life to be poisoned.

FOUR

Tradition Expressed in Different Ways

W ITH THE PASSAGE OF TIME it became important for the
nation of Israel to express her life in writing. Since
Israel was a religious nation, her history is essentially
religious history. A wealth of material developed: Israel's
history books, including that extraordinary group that I call
para-historical, for they contain facts but were not written as
history; her prophetic tradition; and her wisdom tradition,
including the Psalms.

THE HISTORY BOOKS

The history books include Joshua, Judges, Ruth, 1 and 2
Samuel, and 1 and 2 Kings. In the Hebrew Bible these are
called the "early prophets." The "later prophets" comprise
Isaiah, Jeremiah, and the other recognized prophets. Joshua
was credited with the book bearing his name, Samuel with
the Book of Judges and those of Samuel, and Jeremiah with
the Books of Kings.

These books are not to be seen as historical in the sense of
secular history today, for they relate religious history. That

is, they speak about the relationship of God to a people covenanted to him by a sacred and unbreakable bond, which shaped their history in a way that was unique among the nations. The authors are mainly concerned with Israel's obedience to God and the Covenant on the personal, social, and political levels. Their judgment of the individual, the king, and the nation is based on this. They do relate historical facts, but their primary interest in dealing with history lies in the religious life of the people.

There is a very close connection between the Book of Deuteronomy and these historical books. The influence of D is extensive in Judges and in Kings, but less so in Samuel. Deuteronomy lays out the doctrine for the election of Israel as God's special people, a theocratic nation. Joshua illustrates Israel establishing herself as such a nation, while Judges recounts her many defections and falls from grace. The Books of Samuel deal with the crisis that led to the foundation of the monarchy and its growing pains, while the Books of Kings relate the decline of the monarchy.

The D school appears to be behind this literature. This school would have consisted of prophets, scribes, wise men, teachers, and priests, all profoundly influenced by the teaching of Deuteronomy and reflecting their judgment of history from this unique standpoint. They would have had both oral tradition and written documents to work with. For instance, they had access to the annals of the royal houses of Israel and Judah, as well as the scrolls of the prophets and wise men. Nevertheless, the material reflects a single hand at its final stage. The scholars choose to call this person the final editor. Perhaps he was the chief priest or the head of the prophets or the chief wise man at the time. What we do know is that a lot of meticulous work and careful discernment went into the production of the final material that we now call the historical books. Again the names Joshua and Samuel reflect the authority behind the events related, as in the case of Moses and the Pentateuch.

Works of the Chronicler. The Books of Chronicles, Ezra, and Nehemiah are also historical books. This group appears to come from one source. The Chronicles duplicate the work of the Books of Kings, but in a more idealized way. The chronicler has his own way of looking at events and is unafraid to differ from the conclusions of the authors of the Kings. The Chronicles come from the post-exilic era, when the priests were the leaders, the law was the rule of life, and the temple was the center of national life. So this document appears to come from Levitical sources late in Israel's history. The author has a great interest in the temple cult, in God's people as a worshiping community. The chronicler uses other biblical books as sources, especially Genesis, Numbers, Samuel, and Kings (without naming them), as well as the annals of kings, prophets, and wise men.

It is instructive to compare the way Kings and Chronicles deal with the same historical facts. Contrast the idealized presentation of David and his dynasty in the First Book of Chronicles with the same history related in the Books of Samuel and Kings. The chronicler decided to leave out anything that would discredit the founder of the messianic dynasty, the one who succeeded, after Moses, in forming Israel into the theocratic worshiping community that God wanted. To this end he omits David's years as an outlaw, his struggle for power, his adultery with Bathsheba, and the very real family troubles that he endured. Nathan's prophecy regarding David's dynasty is repeated but in a more personalized way; it is "one of David's sons," as distinct from his offspring, who will be the Messiah (1 Chr 17:11-14). The splendors of David's reign are not just a thing of the past but a pledge of a glorious future for God's people. The whole history of David, then, is a prophetic forecast of the coming days of the Messiah. One can understand why the chronicler omits David's sinfulness, for that would not apply to the Coming One!

Ezra and Nehemiah are a continuation of the chronicler's

work. In them he resumes the history of Israel after the Exile, beginning with the edict of Cyrus in 538 B.C. These books are very important as an account of the restoration of the people, the temple, and the cult after the Exile. They are unique insofar as they actually quote from contemporary documents as sources of information. For example, they use lists of returned exiles and the Acts of the Kings of Persia. This is important evidence for the historicity of the events related. The chronicler also uses the personal memoirs of Ezra and Nehemiah to put his work together, and of course, these are the two authorities behind the restoration.

The Books of the Maccabees should be listed here with the historical books, but since they were written late in Israel's history, they are listed with the deuterocanonical books.

The Para-Historical Books. Under the heading of history books we find Ruth, Tobit, Judith, and Esther. These can be called special cases, for they are documents based on some historical facts but are not history in the modern sense.

Scholars are inclined to think of Ruth as we would consider an historical novel today. The historical details are true, but the story is told to teach a lesson or to present an unpalatable truth. In this case the author wants to illustrate the universal love of the Lord, which extends even to those hated or rejected by Israel. It is a story about faith in divine providence being rewarded by God. It also speaks of the origins of David's dynasty, that it had foreign elements as well as those of Israel.

This book is found among the writings in the Hebrew Scriptures. Neither its authorship nor date of composition are known. The book itself says that it is was written "in the days when the judges were governing" (Ru 1:1). However, some scholars feel that it must be later in origin, for like the book of Jonah, it extends God's love to Gentiles, thus preparing the way for the New Testament. If this book had in fact been written during the time of Ezra and Nehemiah, for example, Ruth's position as an ancestor of David would have been a strong correction to the mandate found in these books to put away foreign women. Scholars have resolved the problem by assuming that the basic story was known and taught orally for centuries before its final composition.

Tobit, Judith, and Esther form a small literary group of their own, with distinctive characteristics. Tobit and Judith are deuterocanonical: that is, they were not in the Hebrew canon but were accepted by the church as part of the Septuagint or Greek Bible that was the Old Testament for the early church. Esther was part of the Hebrew canon, but its Greek additions are deuterocanonical. Tobit is not an historical book but more like a romantic novel that teaches about family life, prayer, trust in God, and good works, all of which have enduring value.

Judith is also a dramatic fictional novel that exhibits a bland indifference to both history and geography. The authorship and date of composition are unknown. Its purpose is to teach certain lessons. Judith, the holy widow, models right relationship with God. She leads her people to victory through her faith in God and her fearlessness in the face of a human foe. Her faith gives her more courage than all the men in the town, and she becomes a glory to Israel and a model for all.

Judith is an unusual woman who is not afraid to challenge the thinking of her own day. It was unheard of for a woman to execute a man, for instance! It was also most unusual for a woman to correct the thinking of national or religious leaders (8:9-34). Further, women did not refuse to marry (16:22), nor did they manage their own affairs. Judith is presented as an independent woman who takes her full place in society, shoulder-to-shoulder with the men.

The Book of Esther also tells of the deliverance of the nation by a woman who puts her trust in God and is fearless in the face of a foreign foe. In this case the enemy is Esther's husband! This tale of heroism was retold down through the centuries and "grew," as commentary was added to the narrative. The story illustrates the hatred directed towards the Jews in ancient times because their unique way of life brought them into conflict with autocratic kings.

This story bears strong resemblance to that of the patriarch Joseph, for he too rose to a high position in a foreign court and used his influence to save his own people. In both cases God makes no outward manifestation of his power, yet he directs events as the Lord of history.

God is central to the Book of Esther, yet no one meets him or claims any particular closeness to him. The story confirms the faith of "little people," for God genuinely hears the cry of the poor and afflicted and takes up their cause. God works quietly in the background so that only those who pray know of his intervention. This book is thought to have been finalized in the second century B.C., and came to be associated with the Feast of Purim (9:20-32).

THE PROPHETIC BOOKS

The Old Testament canon is divided into three sections, the Law, the Prophets, and the Writings. We have looked at authorship of the first section, the Pentateuch, in chapter 2; now we consider the second group.

We have already noted that the Hebrew Bible put the historical books under the heading of the "early prophets." Now we come to consider the "later prophets," namely Isaiah, Jeremiah, and Ezekiel, who are called the major prophets, and the so-called minor prophets who are described in "the book of the twelve." (Major and minor have to do with the length of the books, not with the relative importance of the prophet's teaching.) The Book of Daniel came late on the scene and is put at the end of the Hebrew canon. He is treated under the heading of apocalyptic rather than prophetic writing.

The historical books were included among the prophets

because they are not just a record of facts; they contain a prophetic interpretation of history (see 2 Mc 2:25-26). These books also present many important prophets and their ministries—for example, Samuel, Nathan, Ahijah, Elijah, Elisha, Miciah ben Imlah, and other prophetic figures, including women such as Deborah and Huldah.

The "later prophets" are the books that we more readily designate as prophetic books, for they contain the oracles and teachings of the prophets for whom they are named. They are often called the classical prophets, for in them prophecy reached its high point. Sometimes they are called the writing prophets, although this is less apt.

Israel's prophets are an extraordinary group by any standards. As the spiritual leaders of the nation, they helped to preserve its faith, especially in time of crisis. Without them Israel would not have survived and the Bible would never have been written. Their contribution to the Bible goes far beyond the actual books attributed to them, for it is their interpretation of history that is presented in the historical books.

Initially the scribes and annalists of Israel only preserved memoirs and scattered pronouncements of the earlier prophets. These are found in the books of Samuel and Kings. But by the eighth century B.C.; the scribes began to appreciate the importance of the prophets in the mystery of the relationship between God and the nation. The prophets were God's spokesmen; they revealed the Word of God to Israel in a very personal and immediate way. Having arrived at this discernment, the scribes kept more detailed and accurate accounts of the lives and times of the various prophets. The prophetic schools also kept records, for they had realized long before the nation as a whole did, the importance of the prophets in the communication of God's Word. The classical prophets also formed disciples who would continue their teaching after they were gone, thus ensuring continuity (Is 8:16).

It is now evident that the prophets were not writers. They

were missionary preachers "on the road" all the time. They dealt with live audiences and were totally taken up with the problems of their mission. A reading of their text reveals that some material is given in the first person, but much of it is related in the third person. Some of the text consists of oracles or predictions given by the prophets themselves, some is made up of the prophets' own diary or memoirs, and some is obviously the work of an editor or compiler.

Jeremiah dictated what he wanted preserved to his scribe Baruch (Jer 36:4). This work took twenty-three years, but the king just burnt it when it was presented to him (Jer 36:23)! Afterwards Baruch wrote another scroll, this time adding biographical details of the prophet (Jer 37-44).

Similar circumstances probably lie behind the composition of the other books, with some involvement on the part of the prophet himself. Isaiah committed his teaching to his disciples for preservation (Is 8:16).

The prophets' oracles and teaching were preserved in the prophetic schools, where they were kept safely for centuries and passed on to the next generation. This would explain the similarities between the middle and final sections of the Book of Isaiah, which are called Deutero-Isaiah or Second Isaiah, and sometimes Trito-Isaiah or Third Isaiah. These come from a different age from that found in the first thirty-nine chapters of the book.

Disciples or scribes gathered various oracles under a particular heading, such as "the oracles against the nations," thus beginning the process of collections of oracles. The finished book would then be the work of the final editor, who put the various collections together along with other teachings of the prophet and some biographical and auto-biographical material, which would have come from the prophetic schools. Sometimes the final editors included anonymous oracles in the book in order to preserve them also. In this way less well-known prophets would have their oracles preserved for posterity.

A similar type of publishing goes on today when a

person's works are collected, edited, and published, often posthumously. This final book is based on the works of the person concerned and includes all of his work, but it also contains material belonging to the compiler and editor of the finished work. Anthologies of poetry are like this.

THE WISDOM TRADITION

This body of literature contains the Books of Job, Psalms, Proverbs, Ecclesiastes, the Song of Songs, Wisdom, and Sirach. Since neither Psalms nor the Song fit this category very well, we shall deal with them in the last part of this section.

The sages of Israel were a distinct body of scholars. They were not only in touch with life at its grass roots and able to teach about it, but they also had contact with sages all over the Mediterranean world and learned from them. These sages are even quoted. The wisdom of Agur and Lemuel, men who came from Massa, a tribe in northern Arabia (Gn 25:14) is found in Proverbs 30 and 31. Whole psalms are attributed to Heman and Ethan, who were famous Canaanite sages, men who deserved to be mentioned among the great teachers that Israel listened to (1 Kgs 5:11).

Wisdom literature flourished throughout the various cultures of the ancient Near East. The "wise men" came from the east, from Mesopotamia, to share their insights into life and its meaning with all who would listen. Job had his three wise men from the east also, although one could question their wisdom in dealing with the inexplicable sufferings of their neighbor. Even Matthew's Gospel has the wise men coming from the east to share with Israel their newfound revelation regarding the imminent birth of the King of the Jews. And we are informed by Matthew that they were specifically guided by God in their search for the infant king.

Although secular wisdom interested itself in the "good

life'' and all that would make life more successful, the sages of Israel brought their unique faith in God to bear on this type of research into the meaning of life. For them, wisdom dealt with more than how to conduct one's personal and social affairs towards success. It had a specifically religious dimension, for only the Lord knew his people as the potter knows the clay. They saw that wisdom was an attribute of God and that all true wisdom came from God. The very root of wisdom lay in the fear of the Lord. This is not servile fear, but an adult appraisal of God's greatness and holiness, compared to the sinfulness of the human condition and our consequent unworthiness to walk with God. True wisdom calls for obedience to God as the rule of life. The discipline of doing God's will is what brings us to maturity.

Solomon. Solomon, the son of David, was Israel's greatest sage and the patron of the wisdom movement. He is to wisdom literature what Moses is to the Law and David is to the Psalter. The Books of Kings attribute to Solomon the solution to the problem of which of the two women brought before him was the dead infant's mother (1 Kgs 3:16-28). This story was an ancient "whodunnit," given to test the wisdom of many a great man besides Solomon. The First Book of Kings uses it to prove Solomon's wisdom and authority. Solomon is said to have surpassed the wisdom of the east, which in modern parlance is equivalent to saying that he had wisdom in its highest degree.

Solomon is supposed to have composed three thousand proverbs and to have written one thousand songs. He was able to hold discourses on many scientific matters that were a wonder in his day (1 Kgs 5:9-14). His wisdom began with a personal meeting with God in which he knew to ask not for temporal things but for the gifts needed to carry out his duties as God's vice regent (1 Kgs 3:4-15). It is to this man that the wisdom books of Israel are dedicated, even though, in their final form, they were compiled and edited about four hundred years after Solomon's time. These books contain Solomon's wisdom, but they also include the works of other sages.

The wisdom teachers found their natural place in society in the schools. In Solomon's time that probably meant the court, where the teachers trained crown princes, nobles, scribes, and other potential leaders for their future roles in society. The highest principles of ethics and religion were taught, as well as how to conduct themselves both in private and in public matters. As leaders, they would have to know how to deal with the poor, the lowly, and the needy, as was laid down by Moses. Here, of course, the teachings of the prophets meet those of the sages. We do not know if the schools of the prophets and those of the sages were different. If they were, then they certainly learned from each other, for one can see the mutual influence of the sages and the prophets in their writings.

The Book of Proverbs is an anthology of Wisdom literature. The author is responsible for the long introduction, chapters 1 through 9, in which wisdom is personified and prophetically calls everyone to follow God and thus find happiness and fulfillment. These chapters influenced the Gospel of John in presenting Jesus as wisdom incarnate.

This introduction is followed by various collections of wisdom sayings that had come from the schools. There are two collections of Solomon, in chapters 10 through 22 and 25 through 29.

The Book of Sirach, although written in the second century B.C., comes from an ancient source. The author identifies himself as one Jesus Ben Sira (or Sirach in Greek). This Jerusalem sage and teacher gives us his deep reflections on the Scriptures and on life itself. His grandson took his book back to Egypt, where it was translated into Greek. Ben Sira also personifies wisdom and continuously praises her. Wisdom is identified with God and is God's gift to us. The sage also gives a long eulogy on Israel's famous ancestors

(Sir 44-50), in which he shows that the sages meditated on God's saving events of history and learned from them.

Reflections on Suffering. The Book of Ecclesiastes looks at the problems of life. The author is Qoheleth, a name that apparently reveals him as a master or leader of a school of sages. He is a very pessimistic writer, from the fourth or third century B.C., who feels that it does not make any difference whether you are wise or not, for "all is vanity"! Since possessing knowledge does not, of itself, make one happy or successful, he is convinced that "out there somewhere" a law of retribution is at work that we can do nothing about. Looking at human experience, he asks what the point is in laboring for so much knowledge, money, or even experience, when we all end up in the grave anyway! He gives only limited value to anything human. Life, he says, has inevitable suffering over which we, as individuals, have no control. We can only endure, and God seems very silent. He feels helpless before the forces that govern the universe.

Qoheleth's candid but pessimistic view of life has value, and not just for those who are suffering. His whole book argues for the need for an afterlife. Such a belief would have solved a lot of his problems, especially that of the just man dying at the hands of others, while the wicked flourish.

Both Ecclesiastes and Job look at the meaning of suffering in the light of retribution. Both reject the current solutions, yet the books are very different in character. The author of Job is a poet who does not stand off from his subject but gets passionately involved. In fact, he sounds very much like one who has suffered and triumphed in his own life, one who wants to share the treasures with others. Qoheleth, on the other hand, sounds like a dispassionate philosopher who speaks theoretically on this painful subject. Yet the subject does not yield to book answers but only to contemplation.

Job is one of the literary masterpieces of all time and deserves to be studied as such, even apart from its wonderful subject. The narrative section at the beginning and end of the book concerns a famous legendary figure, whose story forms the framework for this poet to give us his profound insights into life. He tells us in chapters 38 through 42 that only a more profound experience of God in his transcendent greatness can solve life's riddle.

Daniel Deals with Difficulty. Those who claim that biblical faith is an invention of humans searching for a blessed immortality are given the lie in the wisdom books. These books continuously teach on how to live a good life, and get the most out of our time on earth. Exact knowledge of what happens after death came only very slowly. The ancient world spoke vaguely about a survival of the spirit in Sheol or Hades. After the Exile, knowledge of the resurrection of the dead came mainly through Daniel 12:2 when Israel's faith had been tried and tested for centuries. It is worth noting that Israel put her trust in the Lord and tried to follow his difficult demands without the prospect of reward in an afterlife! Hence the struggle we find in the Psalms as people try to respond to this heroic faith (see Psalm 88, for example). The struggle in the Books of Job and Ecclestiastes to understand a good God in the very difficult areas of unmerited suffering and injustice would lead the discerning reader to conclude that "the books could only be balanced" in an afterlife where good would be rewarded and evil punished.

Then came the very severe test of the persecution of Antiochus IV Epiphanes, who in the second century B.C. set out to destroy Judaism. Those who remained faithful were killed, while others escaped death by apostasy. This made the people consider that if there were no afterlife, the apostates were better off than those who remained faithful to the Lord! This could not be if God were a just God, and they sought him in prayer for a solution. The Book of Daniel, which appeared about this time, deals with the problem. The Book of Daniel proclaimed the resurrection of the dead

(Dn 12:2), thus revealing ultimate justice in the Kingdom of God. The Books of the Maccabees also came from this period, and they too proclaimed the eternal reward of the just and the punishment of the wicked. The martyrdom of the seven sons in 2 Maccabees 7 celebrates this revelation of eternal life for the just who remained faithful to God (also see 2 Mc 6).

The fact that this new revelation came only in response to the search for meaning in a difficult situation shows the progressive nature of revelation, as God responds to the felt needs of his children. God had prepared an eternal reward for us *anyway*. Faced with the near prospect of martyrdom, Israel sought God and discovered that his plan for the human race surpassed all previous expectations. This was an important preparation for the gospel.

The Book of Wisdom. It was at this new stage of development that the Book of Wisdom appeared. It was composed in Greek by an Alexandrian Jew in the first century B.C. Steeped in the Jewish faith, this man wanted to save his people from the inroads of paganism, for Alexandria, in Egypt, was the chief city of Hellenism under the Ptolemies (323-63 B.C.) and was the home of many Jews of the Diaspora.

The book is usually called the Wisdom of Solomon, however, for the author writes as if he were a king (7:5; 8:9-15) addressing his fellow kings (1:1; 6:1-11). This is obviously a literary device. Evidence that Solomon did not personally write the book comes from the fact that when the author quotes from Scripture he uses the Septuagint, the Greek translation, which came from these circles about this time also.

Wisdom is said to have been finally published around 50 B.C. It influenced John's Gospel in his presentation of Jesus as incarnate wisdom. It also influenced Paul's description of Jesus as the one in whom the fullness of wisdom and knowledge are found (Col 2:2).

The author is concerned with the idea of retribution. In chapter 2 he describes the thoughts and ways of the wicked, then goes on to proclaim a day of reckoning for them and reward for the just. This day is what Christians would term "the Last Judgment" (3:10-12; 4:18-5:14). Therefore there is a death worse than physical death and a life more wonderful than life on earth. In the light of an eternal destiny, earthly matters bear new scrutiny. Barrenness, celibacy (which Qumran monks practiced at this time), and early death, which were considered tragedies in the past, have new meaning (3:13-4:15).

Chapters 6 through 9 deal with the origin and nature of wisdom itself. Wisdom comes from God alone. We gain it through prayer, and it is the ultimate source of all our good. The author's description of wisdom in 7:22-8:1 is about the best answer that can be given to the question, "Who is the Holy Spirit?"

The third section of the book is an inspired commentary on Scripture, usually called *Midrash* by scholars. Here the author deals with wisdom's role in the whole history of Israel. One could just as easily say "the role of the Spirit of God" in guiding and governing his people's destiny.

The Songs of Israel. The Psalms are an anthology of songs, poems, and hymns representing the liturgy of Israel during most of her history. The whole collection of psalms is attributed to David, although he is the author of eighty-two psalms at the most (seventy-three are attributed to him in the Hebrew Bible, and eighty-two in the Septuagint). Other authors who are acknowledged in the Psalter are Heman, Ethan, Moses, Solomon, and the Sons of Korah. The majority of authors are anonymous, however.

The Psalter as we have it today was put together by the Jerusalem priests from various collections of psalms that were in use at that time. As one might expect, many psalms were lost with the passage of time. Recent discoveries have revealed new psalms to us, such as Psalm 151 from the Dead Sea Scrolls.

The editors put the Psalter together thematically, arranging it in five books to parallel the Pentateuch. Thus many of the themes one finds in the various parts will have their counterpart in the corresponding book of the Pentateuch. For example, Psalm 1 deals with the two ways an individual can live: God's way or his own way. Genesis 2 and 3 deal with this same choice. In Psalm 2 nations also must choose, so the earth houses two camps, as in Genesis 4 through 7. The fate of the good and the wicked is dealt with in many psalms, as is the persecution of the good by the wicked.

Themes of the Fall and the need for Redemption are dealt with in the first section (Pss 1-41), while themes of Redemption and the Redeemer are dealt with in section 2 (Pss 42-72). The third section (Pss 73-89) parallels Leviticus with its emphasis on liturgy, worship, and the need for holiness.

The fourth section (Pss 90-106) corresponds to Numbers. It begins with the only Psalm of Moses in the Psalter (the man of the wilderness), and closes with a recounting of Israel's failures in the wilderness. These psalms reveal the failure of God's people to respond faithfully to his election and grace.

The final section (Pss 107-150) concerns God and his Word. In a way these psalms recall the teaching of the other sections of the Psalter. They tell us that all blessing for us, as individuals or nations, is bound up with obedience to God's Word. Disobedience, on the other hand, is the cause of ruin, both for the individual and society. The longest psalm, Psalm 119, says twelve times, "By your Word give us life!" Part 5 ends with five psalms of praise, so that the Psalter ends where Heaven begins.

It seems that David may have been responsible for a new development in the liturgy of his people since he was an excellent musician and songwriter (1 Sm 16:16-18; 2 Sm 1:19-

27; 3:33-34). He had a great love of the liturgy, and he brought the ark to Jerusalem (2 Sm 6:5-16). He made himself famous for many things, not least as the "singer of the songs of Israel" (2 Sm 23:1).

The impulse given by David ensured that Israel would never lack poets and songwriters, as the Psalter testifies. First Chronicles 25:1 states that Asaph, Heman, and Jeduthun, who were put in charge of the liturgy in the temple, were orderd to "prophesy to the accompaniment of harps, lyres, and cymbals."

A Love Song. The Song of Songs is the greatest of all songs, one which celebrates human love. It is attributed to Solomon, although neither the authorship nor date of composition are known. It consists of a series of love songs put together to make a greater work. Some say that the songs were written at an earlier date and then put together in final form after the Exile, but there is as yet no conclusive proof for this theory.

The Song has been variously interpreted. Today scholars favor the literal interpretation—that it celebrates human love and its effects on the growth of the individual. The procreative side of love is not dealt with in these romantic songs, which concentrate on the relationship between lover and beloved. As such, it has much to say on the wholesomeness of marriage and human love. The traditional Christian interpretation has been to view the Song as celebrating the love between Christ and his church, as well as the love between Christ and the individual. This love leads to our redemption here on earth, and our final transformation in glory.

Part II

The Problem of Authenticity

FIVE

The Divine Author

B ELIEVERS CLAIM that God is the origin of revelation in the Scriptures, that he is the divine author of this vast library that we know of as the Old Testament and New Testament. This means that the Word of God truly comes to us through the words of men.

The Vatican Council affirmed the church's teaching on the inspiration of the Scriptures. The "Dogmatic Constitution on Divine Revelation," (3:11) reads: "Those divinely revealed realities which are contained and presented in sacred Scripture have been committed to writing under the inspiration of the Holy Spirit. Holy Mother Church, relying on the belief of the apostles, holds that the books of both the Old and New Testament in their entirety, with all their parts, are sacred and canonical because, having been written under the inspiration of the Holy Spirit ... they have God as their author and have been handed on as such to the church herself."

EVIDENCE IN THE SCRIPTURES

There is some evidence in the New Testament that the earliest disciples of Jesus and the early church officially held to the doctrine of the divine inspiration of the Scriptures.

One of the most important of these texts is 2 Timothy 3:14-17. Here Paul tells the young bishop to "remember who your teachers were, and how, ever since you were a child, you have known the holy Scriptures—from these you can learn the wisdom that leads to salvation through faith in Christ Jesus. All Scripture is inspired by God and useful for refuting error, for guiding people's lives and teaching them to be holy. This is how someone dedicated to God becomes fully equipped and ready for any good work."

The Holy Scriptures that Paul refers to here is the Old Testament, since the New Testament was only in the second stage of formation by then. "All Scripture" therefore refers to the three main sections of the Old Testament, namely the Law (Torah), the Prophets, and the Writings. It includes both the earliest and the latest of God's revelations to Israel.

Jesus made it clear to the two disciples on the road to Emmaus (Lk 24:27, 44) that they could only understand him in reference to the already revealed Word of God, since Jesus himself was the fulfillment of the Scriptures. Jesus, therefore, is the key to understanding the Scriptures. Without that key they do not hang together.

Another important piece of internal evidence is 2 Peter 1:19-21 and 3:15-16. In the first instance Peter, aware of his impending death, is anxious that the church stand on a sure foundation in her faith. He reminds her that he was with Jesus on Mount Tabor, here referred to as the holy mountain. The visitation of God on that mountain was, for Peter, James, and John, their Christian "Sinai." There they met God face-to-face in and through Jesus. They also had an exalted vision of Moses and Elijah, who spoke of Jesus' passing as a fulfillment of the Scriptures (Lk 9:31). There God spoke to the Apostles, instructing them to listen to Jesus and follow him from that moment.

As we read this Letter of Peter, written possibly some thirty years after the event, we can still hear the excitement of the author in the realization of his privilege, which was greater than that given to Moses. The transfiguration of Jesus was a preliminary glimpse of the fulfillment of Scripture, so the author goes on in 2 Peter 1:19-21 to affirm that all prophecy in the Old Testament comes from God. He says, "No prophecy ever came from human initiative. When people spoke for God it was the Holy Spirit that moved them."

In 2 Peter 3:15-16 the author comments on Paul's letters, which were in circulation throughout the churches. The surprise is that he refers to Paul's writings as Scripture! This means that at a very early date the church accepted Paul as one of those men whom the Holy Spirit used to teach his Word. The author of Peter refers to difficult passages in Paul's letters which "uneducated and unbalanced people distort, in the same way as they distort the rest of Scripture—to their own destruction."

John 20:30-31 states that "there were many other signs that Jesus worked in the sight of the disciples, but they are not recorded in this book. These are recorded so that you may believe that Jesus is the Christ, the Son of God, and that believing this you may have life through his name." Here John shows that the Holy Spirit guided him in his selection of the material circulating among believers. He chose only incidents that the Holy Spirit considered pertinent to explaining the person and mission of Jesus the Savior. Therefore the Holy Spirit helped him with both text and commentary (a point we will come back to later).

The purpose of the selection was clear. Only the Lord knew which incidents would reveal the saving events best. He thus preserved the authors from just giving us reminiscences rather than the coherent evaluation that they, in fact, left us. John says that the purpose of his gospel was to impart a *living knowledge* of Jesus Christ to his readers. By entering into this living relationship with Jesus we receive the grace offered to anyone who reads—and especially prays—John's text.

Other New Testament texts that assert the inspiration of the Scriptures are Matthew 22:43 and Mark 12:36. Both of these texts assert that Jesus asked the Pharisees, "Then how is it that David, moved by the Spirit, calls him Lord?" This reference to Psalm 110:1 asserts the inspiration of the Psalter as a whole. The Holy Spirit is said to have spoken through David in Acts 1:16-20, where the early church finds fulfillment of a prophecy in the Psalms in the fate of Judas. The Psalms are quoted as God's Word here.

In Acts 28:25 Paul says that the Holy Spirit spoke through the prophet Isaiah, and he sees the present events as the fulfillment of what Isaiah had prophesied some eight hundred years before. God is said to have spoken through the prophets in general in Luke 1:70 and through Moses in Mark 12:26. Last but not least, Peter teaches in 1 Peter 1:10-12 that the Spirit who spoke through the prophets was *"the Spirit of Christ* bearing witness in them . . . revealing the sufferings of Christ and the glories to follow them."

Before the Christian era the people of Israel had held for close to a thousand years that the holy books were the work of God. Some texts assert that the writers or revealers of the Word, if they were the prophets as distinct from those who wrote down their message, were inspired by the Holy Spirit. Hence Hosea 1:2 asserts that God had spoken through the prophet Hosea, and 2 Samuel 23:2 says that God spoke through David, the son of Jesse. (So both Testaments attest to David's inspiration by God.) The Babylonian Talmud (the Jewish commentary on Scripture coming from the communities that stayed in Babylon after the Exile) affirms that the Torah is divinely revealed. It asserts that since all the great prophets beginning with Moses were taught by God, then their writings are of divine origin also (Dt 15:15-18; Ex 15:20-21; 2 Chr 15:1-5).

Since Isaiah 11:2 tells us that the gifts of the Holy Spirit that God wished to bestow on his holy servant contained also "the spirit of wisdom and insight, the spirit of counsel and power, the spirit of knowledge and fear of the Lord," then one must agree that the writings of the sages (the wisdom writers) were also inspired by the Holy Spirit.

The early church fathers accepted the inspiration of the Scriptures as almost self-evident. They quote the Scriptures to give weight to their teaching, and their writings cover the expanse of both Testaments. For example, Clement (A.D. 150-215) wrote about "sacred writings" and holy books, affirming that the authors were inspired. Origen (A.D. 185-254) did the same.

WHAT DOES "INSPIRED" MEAN?

It is one thing to assert that the sacred Scriptures are inspired, it is quite another matter to explain what is meant by that apparently simple statement! Since we know that each book of the Bible has a long history of development, is it the originator of the book or the final editor who is inspired? If the book passed through many hands over the centuries, was every hand inspired? Is the Holy Spirit involved at only one point or at all points? Is he the overseer or the author?

Through the centuries the answers to these questions have changed considerably. The initial idea was that inspiration came by "divine dictation" to the prophet or receiver of the revelation. This was illustrated in the film *The Ten Commandments*, where a shaft of fiery light cut two tablets from stone and then wrote God's Word on them. Good drama, but did Moses receive the revelation like that? Is it not dramatic enough that God would reveal himself to his creatures? Elijah hears God speak "in the still small voice" after the drama of the storm is over (1 Kgs 19:13). God is pure Spirit, and he communicates effectively to the spirit, in the depths of the heart of the prophet or saint. He does not need television drama. Divine inspiration is the work of the Holy Spirit who with the human author communicates what God wants to say.

THE HOLY SPIRIT'S GUIDANCE

By the second century A.D. church fathers like Origen began to realize that God would require the cooperation of the human author, that it was a joint venture between both authors. But how did it work? Even at this early stage they began to distinguish between the revelatory statements of the Gospels and the evangelists' own words or commentary. They held that the Holy Spirit permitted this commentary as part of the inspired text. So the work of both authors was interwoven throughout. The final text is the inspired Word of God.

What is the Word of God for us then? St. Augustine, from the fourth century, said that we must look for the meaning intended by the author the Holy Spirit chose to work with. The same Holy Spirit would guide the reader, as he did the writer, to understand what God is saying through the text. See John 14:26, where we are told that the Holy Spirit will teach us everything and remind us of the Lord's teaching. John 16:13 says that the Holy Spirit is still the prophetic Spirit for the church. He will continue the work of prophecy if we let him work through us.

The Vatican Council asserts in its "Document on Divine Revelation" (3:11) that "in composing the sacred books, God chose men and while employed by him they made use of their powers and abilities, so that with him acting in them, they, as true authors, consigned to writing everything and only those things which he wanted." The text goes on to say that everything asserted by these authors is to be taken as asserted by the Holy Spirit himself.

The notion that the Scriptures were dictated to the authors has been held by many right up to the present day, despite the exhaustive research that has been done in textual criticism. It seems that little of this scholarly research finds its way into the hands of the average Christian. Many people view the work of scholars with suspicion anyway, thinking that they are trying to destroy the Scriptures rather than illuminate them. The prophetic theory of inspiration is persistent also; it has carried the church through the Middle Ages, the Reformation, and the Counter-Reformation, right up to today.

The church adds that the Bible is inspired, but she does not claim to explain adequately the mysterious workings of God with his creatures. When any text of the Bible is read in church, the affirmation "This is the Word of God" is given immediately after it. Yet a passage in a Gospel has a context in that Gospel. That Gospel has its context in the whole New Testament, which finds its explanation in the context of the whole Bible, and the context in which the Bible as a whole is explained is the faith of the church in the church. Today scholars are aware of the need for a holistic approach to understanding inspiration and to finding the true meaning of a word or text in any part of the Bible. Inspiration must include the specifics of this and also the wider implications.

THE HUMAN ELEMENT

Nowadays we realize that it is possible to be inspired by the Holy Spirit without knowing it. It was not necessary that a writer be aware of what the divine author was doing through his writing. Sometimes we can be used by God to help another person without being aware of a specific inspiration at the time. Everything is clearer in retrospect when we examine what happened and its consequences.

Take Psalm 88 as an example. The author was facing death from a loathsome disease that isolated him from friends and family. He did not have the revelation of eternal life, and he cried out to God in his pain. Using poetic exaggeration, he said that he was in prison and could not escape, that he was down among the dead, cut off from life. If you take his psalm and compare it with the events of Holy Thursday; there is a striking resemblance to what happened to Jesus when the psalm was perfectly fulfilled without exaggeration. It was not necessary that the author would be aware that the Holy Spirit was thinking of a different sufferer than himself. The sufferings of this unknown man foreshadowed the sufferings of that other man, who is said to be universally known but who is truly unknown (in the real sense) by most. (See *Words of Life: Psalms of Praise* by Frances Hogan, for fuller commentary.)

Scholarship today is very aware of the human element in the sacred writings. The inspired authors used very ordinary methods of communication. Luke, for instance, said that he had done a lot of research before undertaking to write his Gospel. He studied both written accounts and oral testimony before setting out to give a different presentation of the Christ event (Lk 1:1-2). All of this is part of the inspirational process in the Gospel. Luke did not rely on the "verbal dictation" of the Holy Spirit. Like all responsible authors, he researched his material before writing. Nevertheless, he was specifically aided by the Holy Spirit in that work, so much so that the Holy Spirit can also be said to be an author of Luke's work.

The author of 2 Maccabees says that his work was no easy task but a matter of sweat and burning the midnight oil (2 Mc 2:25-26). He goes on to explain why and how he wrote his work, saying that while he wrote about historical facts, he did not intend to be an historian. It is important to remember this when reading his work.

One can see then that the Bible can be approached as a purely human work, and it is often studied as such today. Even at this level it is acknowledged as the world's greatest library, since it has influenced the western world profoundly in all its institutions, both social and political. It has also influenced its art, drama, and literature. The Book of Job, for example, is one of the world's greatest classics, dealing with the unanswerable problems of suffering. The prophets of the Bible still cry out to us concerning social justice, and call the nations back to faith in God.

For the believer, the Bible is all this and much more, for it is the very Word of God. In it the Lord speaks directly about all that concerns us and our world, with the same urgency as always, and the same infinite love.

SIX

Discernment of the Canon

THE SAVING EVENTS OF GOD in both the Old and New Testament produced an enormous amount of writing from various sources. Some authority had to decide which writings were important to the community's life, which were inspired by the Holy Spirit, and therefore to be incorporated forever (canonized) into the sacred collection of writings that we call the Bible.

APPLYING THE MEASURING ROD

The word *canon* derives from the Hebrew *kanon*, which originally meant a measuring rod. With usage it came to be regarded as a rule or standard of excellence, the "norm." Discernment was vital for deciding which books were truly given by God, as distinct from the volumes of material presented by good people in order to help the community of believers. The decision was not made by referendum but by consensus and usage, under the guidance of the God-appointed leaders of the community.

Those books which were canonized by the believing

community were the ones considered to have a special authority in regulating the spiritual life of the nation (for Israel) and of the church (for Christians). They were considered to have God's own teaching regarding faith and morals, and were to be taken as authoritative for guiding the people in holiness (2 Tm 3:16). The saints of both Testaments serve as proof that the books of the Bible were discerned well. These men and women based their lives on the teaching of the holy books. They grew in holiness and became the instruments of God for their own generation. Their great feats of courage and service to God and humanity continue to inspire us today. Like John the Baptist, they were lamps shining in a dark place, leading others to God and life (Jn 5:35).

For us Christians, the discernment of the early church fathers is vital in deciding what is Scripture and what is just human writing. The earliest witness to the *complete* collection of all Scripture is found in the writings of Anthonasius, circa A.D. 367. He lists twenty-seven books for the New Testament. Both he and Jerome give twenty-two for the Old Testament. This may seem a surprisingly small number for the Old Testament, but they lumped all twelve minor prophets into one book! They also put "double" books together as one: 1 and 2 Samuel; 1 and 2 Kings; 1 and 2 Chronicles; Ezra-Nehemiah; Jeremiah-Lamentations. When we count each prophet and each double book separately, we come up with the thirty-nine books of the Hebrew Bible.

A further problem is that the Catholic Bible has more books than the Protestant one. Actually the terms "Catholic" and "Protestant" are unsuitable for designating the sacred books which have come down from antiquity, when these terms were unknown. With modern scholarship one hopes that they will be dropped.

The extra books that the Catholic church has canonized are Tobit, Judith, 1 and 2 Maccabees, Wisdom, Sirach,

Baruch, and some parts of both Esther and Daniel. These were not found in the oldest collection of the Hebrew Scriptures, but they are in the Greek translation known as the Septuagint, which was the Bible used by the early church. These books are of later origin, so the church calls them deuterocanonical, meaning, "in the second listing" of the Scriptures. The Protestant churches call these books apocryphal because they do not accept them as inspired. Altogether the Catholic Bible has seventy-three books: in the Old Testament there are five books in the Pentateuch, sixteen historical books, eighteen prophetic books, and seven wisdom books, (a total of forty-six); and the New Testament contains twenty-seven books. The Protestants have seven less books in their Old Testament.

A PROLIFIC CHURCH

We have many other books written between 200 B.C. and A.D. 200. A codex, or book, called Sinaticus was found in St. Catherine's Monastery at the foot of Mount Sinai by Constantin von Tischendorf in 1844. It was an almost complete Greek New Testament written (that is, copied from existing manuscripts) in the fourth century. This discovery was the oldest written copy of the New Testament, and it caused a sensation among scholars and believers alike. But it also included two other writings which are not in our New Testament—namely, the Epistle of Barnabas and the Shepherd of Hermas.

The codex Alexandrinus, another major manuscript, also contains two letters of one of the early church fathers, Clement of Rome. This comes from the time before the canon was finally fixed. Although these new books (and there are many more) were used by the faithful and can still inspire us today, the church did not put them on a par with the rest of Scripture.

It is well-known today that the Gospels do not give us all the teaching and miracles of Jesus. The early church had a vast tradition, out of which it chose certain material to include in the Gospels. John says in his Gospel: "There were many other signs that Jesus worked in the sight of the disciples, but they are not recorded in this book. These are recorded so that you may believe that Jesus is the Christ, the Son of God, and that believing this you may have life through his name" (Jn 20:30-31).

Acts 20:35 gives a saying of Jesus not found elsewhere in the New Testament: "Remember the words of the Lord Jesus, who himself said, 'There is more happiness in giving than in receiving.'" Luke 1:1 says that *many others* had undertaken to draw up accounts of the events surrounding the life and mission of Jesus and they were handed down in the tradition. Luke researched this material when preparing to write his own Gospel.

There was awareness of a vast body of material, which is available to us now in the twentieth century through modern research. Some of these works are called "gospels," but were not accepted as inspired works, even though they are useful for understanding the life and times of the New Testament. There is, for example, the Gospel of the Ebionites, the Gospel of the Hebrews, the Infancy Gospel of Thomas, the Gospel of Peter, and many others.

Modeled on the present Acts of the Apostles, which really only deals with the acts of Peter and Paul, there are books dealing with the acts of the other Apostles—John, Peter, Paul, Andrew, and Thomas. Each of these books aims to show the work of a particular Apostle from the time of the Ascension onwards: their apostolate, miracles, journeys, mission, and martyrdom. The above list is not exhaustive, yet it is enough to demonstrate that the work of discernment done by the Fathers of the church was no small matter.

The early church also had to discern a vast amount of literature belonging to the Old Testament period. The books that they kept as useful but not inspired are collectively called the Apocrypha. The *Didache,* or the Teaching of the Twelve Apostles, was considered of great importance in the early church. But it was relegated to the realm of church teaching rather than Scripture. So the church distinguished early in her history between her own teaching, authoritative though it was, and Scripture, which was accepted as divine revelation. Today all the churches agree on the twenty-seven books of the New Testament canon.

THE OLD AND THE NEW

When and how did all this writing begin? Obviously for the earliest followers of Jesus the term "Scripture" applied exclusively to the Jewish holy books, which they inherited from the Apostles. Then Christians were led by the Holy Spirit to write about the events of salvation through Jesus and its implications for the rest of humanity. As the new writings began to circulate and be accepted as Scripture, Christians started to refer to the Hebrew Scriptures as the Old Testament. They did not want to discard the Jewish books, nor relegate them to second place. They only needed the term for clarification (2 Cor 3:14). Christians will be forever indebted to the Jewish people for giving us the Word of God.

In the years immediately following the Resurrection (A.D. 30-50) there was no urgent need for Christians to write about the unique events surrounding the life and mission of Jesus, for their living witnesses were still with them. Yet we know that the pre-gospel material was shaped at this stage. During this time the Christian message was communicated mostly by word of mouth (Rom 10:14-15). The preaching of the Apostles was vital for the church, for they were the living link with Jesus and with his preaching (1 Cor 15:11). As the church spread to foreign lands, scribes began to write down the Apostles' teachings, so that the young communities of believers could preserve them for posterity while nourishing their own lives with them. Apostolic instruction also came to these far-flung communities in the form of apostolic letters, which were preserved and copied to pass on to other communities (Col 4:16-17). These writings formed the earliest Christian collections from which the evangelists drew.

The other major reason why Christian writing began was to combat heresy. St. Paul's letters abound with corrections of false teaching and incorrect understanding of the Christian message. It was vital for the Apostles to put the record straight during their lifetime, so that the true message would be passed on to future generations of believers.

SORTING THROUGH THE WRITINGS

Some writings of the time were preserved but not considered inspired by the Holy Spirit; others were preserved because they were seen as God-given, even though coming through human agency. What was the criterion for deciding inspiration? It seems that apostolic origin was vital for acceptance, for the Apostles were the chief witnesses to Jesus. The church has held from the beginning that the teaching of the Apostles is the teaching of Christ.

The second factor was the importance of the church to which the letter or work was addressed. This local church treasured these works as Scripture and preserved them for posterity, even copying them for distribution to other communities. This was especially true of those churches which boasted an Apostle as their leader or founder. Thus the churches of Asia Minor preserved the works of Paul and John, while that of Rome preserved the works of Peter and his scribe, Mark, and perhaps also the works of Luke.

The third criterion for the canonization of a book as

Scripture was conformity to the rule of faith. If any writing failed to reflect faithfully the teaching of Jesus and the Apostles, it was rejected as Scripture, even though it might be useful as an historical source or otherwise helpful as a reflection of the times. Some of the books that were eventually accepted into the canon of Scripture had to go through a long scrutiny before final acceptance. This illustrates again the serious discernment of the church in forming the Scriptures.

The debate over Revelation and the Letter to the Hebrews in the early church centered on whether they had been written by an Apostle or were of apostolic origin in the wider sense. Both were accepted as Scripture eventually.

The final decision of the church to include twenty-seven books in the New Testament canon was formally ratified and decreed at the Council of Trent (1545-1563). This council settled the question for Catholics.

SEVEN

Tracking Down Errors

M ANY PEOPLE TODAY ARE TROUBLED by the thought that there could be errors in the Bible or that passages may not mean what they have always understood them to mean. Sometimes irresponsible scholars give rise to such doubts and questions. Sometimes we hear or read material that denies the basic tenets of the Christian faith. A good rule to follow is: When in doubt, go back to the sources.

True theological and faith-filled scholarship is knowledge based on revealed truth. Paul warned that anyone teaching a gospel different than that of the Apostles is anathema (Gal 1:6-9), even if that teacher is an angel from Heaven! This leads us to consider problems of inerrancy and the interpretation of the Bible. Both of these issues are vital to our understanding of Scripture as the Word of God.

WHAT DO WE MEAN BY ERRORS?

The simple answer to the question of errors is that it all depends on what you mean by "errors." Having looked at the way the Old Testament came to be written, it is clear that we cannot call the repetitions and duplicate texts in the Pentateuch errors. It is also clear that in the oral tradition different versions of a story developed according to the needs of a particular place. These differences do not constitute errors. There were different schools of theology that contributed to the richness of the insights of the people into the things of God. When the authors or editors of the books included these insights, it was because they saw that it increased the people's knowledge of God.

The "Dogmatic Constitution on Divine Revelation" (Vat II, ch 3.11) says that "all that the inspired authors, or sacred writers, affirm should be regarded as affirmed by the Holy Spirit, we must acknowledge that the books of Scripture, firmly, and faithfully without error, teach that truth which God, for the sake of our salvation, wished to see confided to the sacred Scriptures." This is the church's teaching on the matter after twenty centuries of Christian discernment.

Biblical inerrancy, then, is the Bible's privilege of never teaching error. Does this mean that every statement in the Bible is a divine teaching? Of course not! The Bible does not always teach. There are many statements in its various books that are there for historical, geographical, poetic, or other reasons. However, whenever a biblical author *intends* to teach us something, then the Holy Spirit intends that too. Everything that the Bible *teaches* is without error, but everything in the Bible is not meant as teaching. Each author was left free by the Lord to express himself according to the ideas of his own day. It is the revelation contained in the Scriptures that is important.

SCIENTIFIC PROBLEMS

Advances in modern science have shown that the Bible is inaccurate in some of its scientific statements. Its authors shared the prescientific worldview of their times. They did not know that the world was round, how rain was made, or how the animal species developed. The picture of the world that is painted in Genesis 1 and 2 is still being drawn by children in the twentieth century. It is how the world appears to the naked eye, with the sky "up there" holding the sun, moon, and stars like lights in a ceiling.

How could the authors of Scripture know more science than their contemporaries? Should this ignorance be a blow to the authority of the Bible? Surely not, for the Bible is not a scientific manual. It is a book of revelation about God, his creatures, and their relationship to him. God allowed our understanding of science to develop slowly over the centuries, but he gave us all that we needed to know him, love him, and serve him throughout all ages. He gave us divine truth.

We have already seen that the authors of the two Creation accounts expressed themselves in very different ways. The authors of Genesis 1 expressed the teaching of God as Creator and Lord according to the simple scientific notions of their day. As they were not teaching science but theology, they are not in error. They would be in error, however, if they gave us wrong teaching about God.

Likewise in the story of the Flood, the authors reveal their ignorance of how rain is produced. Genesis 7 says that "all the springs of the great deep burst through, and the floodgates of heaven opened. And rain fell on the earth." The authors are teaching about divine judgment, not the origins of rain, so they are not in error. Even today we describe torrential rain by saying "the heavens have opened."

When Psalm 19 speaks of the sun running like a champion from one end of heaven to the other, the author is not teaching astronomy. Rather he is saying that God's creation gloriously reveals his presence everywhere. Since the author is a poet, he expresses himself in a poetic way. We use unscientific language in our everyday life even though we are a scientifically sophisticated people. The poet and prophet in us must be allowed expression too! What would the people of the twenty-first century think on hearing our expression "It is raining cats and dogs" or "The sun is not shining today"? If they took us literally, they would not credit us with much scientific understanding!

NAMES AND NUMBERS

If the two genealogies of Christ in the Gospels differ, are the evangelists teaching error? No, but we must try to understand why they would have chosen to give the lists of ancestors that they did. Neither Matthew nor Luke intended to give a complete ancestory of Christ. Even if such knowledge were available, it would be just a boring list of names. Matthew chose to list some important ancestors who proved Christ's claim to the Davidic throne. He also highlighted Jesus as the most important descendant of Abraham.

Matthew deliberately gave this message in three sets of fourteen names. Now, numbers in the Bible carry messages, and there is a number corresponding to each letter of the Hebrew alphabet. The name David is spelled D V D in Hebrew, which leaves out the vowel sounds. The corresponding numbers are $4 + 6 + 4 = 14$. The number 3 represents a blessing, so the message of Matthew's genealogy is, the greatest blessing that God ever sent to us was Jesus, the Son of David.

Luke's purpose was to illustrate Christ as the son of David, son of Abraham, son of Adam, and Son of God. So he gave us a more generalized human genealogy, as he was not concerned about the Davidic dynasty. Luke's intention is to portray the Man-God, who like Adam, has no earthly father but comes directly from God. He is therefore the Second Adam, who will inaugurate a new era for the human race, enabling all of his people to live as sons and daughters of God. Luke's seventy-seven generations also speak of perfection in God's creation of Jesus, since 7 represents perfection.

Some other numbers used frequently with a symbolic meaning are 5, 10, 12, and 40. The number 5 represents the Torah, the five books of the Law. Therefore it becomes a symbol of God's Word. The pool with five porticos in John 5:3 represents all the grace that was available in the Old Testament, which was surpassed by the mercy of God coming through Jesus. There were five loaves and two fish in the feeding of the five thousand. The message here is that the perfect food of God (5 + 2 = 7) is a combination of God's Word in the Scriptures and the gift of Jesus in the Eucharist, represented by the fish.

The number 10 has rich symbolism in Sacred Scripture. For example, there are Ten Commandments to guide our lives in the world. The beast of the apocalyptic writers has ten horns (Dn 7:20; Rv 13:1; 17:7). This represents a world power which dominates for a time.

The number 12 represents the fullness of God's works, so there were twelve Tribes in Israel and twelve Apostles of the Lord, as foundations of the New Israel (see Revelation 21:12-14). The number 40 comes from 8 x 5. Eight represents new life, and 5 the Word of God. This number is usually used to denote a period of time when a person goes to God in prayer to await his word and seek the new life that will follow its acceptance. Examples are the forty days of Moses and Jesus in prayer and the forty years Israel spent in the desert before her entrance into the Promised Land.

HISTORICAL PROBLEMS

Here we are on very important ground, for both the Old Testament and New Testament are based on verifiable historical facts: the Exodus, the Covenant, the Exile and return in the Old Testament; the Christ-Event and the foundation and spread of the church in the New Testament. If these events were not verifiable or were doubtful, then we would be in trouble! Therefore other sources outside the Bible should be able to verify these facts, sources like the annals of kings and the writings of prophets, philosophers, and historians other than those involved in these events. These sources even include the annals of the enemies of God's people. All are important, and all these sources, along with the findings of archeology, have verified the facts on which our faith is based.

The whole Bible is called salvation history because its message rests on these concrete events. Yet, as we have seen in our study of authorship and shall see again when we consider interpretation, some authors of the Bible used these facts not to portray history but to teach the lessons of history. They had the same right to do this as a modern author has to use some of the events of World War II to teach the twentieth century some of the lessons it should learn from it.

MORAL PROBLEMS

Many people are disillusioned by the low moral standards we see in some characters in the Bible, particularly in the Old Testament. Yet it would be unfair to take someone to court in the twentieth century for laws yet to be revealed in the twenty-first century. In the same way, we must be aware of the progressive development of morals in the Bible.

First of all, when the Bible reveals the moral failings of its great heroes, it is just telling us the unvarnished truth, unpalatable though it may be. It avoids the later Christian tendency to paint its saints with untouchable holiness. Biblical heroes are more lovable because of their humanness, whereas we can find it difficult to relate to Christian saints whose biographers were afraid to detail their personal struggles.

The Bible gives us a long list of the sins of the saints. Abraham's lies regarding Sarah, Jacob's deceit, Joseph's boasting of his dreams, Moses' murder of the Egyptian and flight, Samson's carnality, David's adultery with Bathsheba and murder of Uriah, Peter's denials, Paul's quarrel with Barnabas, and so on. This list does not discourage disciples who are struggling with their own sinfulness. It consoles us rather, for we see that God has worked his wonders through fragile clay before, and he will do so again through us.

There are other problems regarding morality. What about polygamy, for example? Abraham, the father of our faith, had two wives, and he treated Hagar rather badly (Gn 16). David had a large harem, and Solomon had one consisting of seven hundred wives and three hundred concubines! One would hope that this was an exaggeration to emphasize the glory of Solomon's reign, for the thought of one man with so many women leaves us cold. This is not our idea of wisdom, and the Bible later shows the demoralizing effect such self-indulgence had on Solomon (1 Kgs 11:1-13).

We are also distressed by the cries of vengeance in the Psalms, Psalm 109:6-19, for example. Equally disturbing are the rules of warfare that demanded that the enemy be put "under the ban," which meant that every man, woman, and child was wiped out. How do we explain these and other incidences?

GOD HAS TO RELATE TO SINNERS

There is an explanation. Humans are slow to listen to God and even slower to obey him. We prefer to take the line of least resistance in moral issues, imitating what everyone else does rather than seeking God's will. God must relate to us as sinners or not at all, for so few of us really carry out his will as he demands. If the revelation of salvation was a very slow process, then that of morality was even slower.

Then there is the fact that sinners find it difficult to live holy lives. They can only do so when graced and guided by God. If we of the twentieth century, who live in the full light of God's salvation and grace, fall short of God's call, how much more difficult must it have been for our Old Testament ancestors, who did not have the full power of Jesus' redemption to help them. We have no excuse, but they have, for they lived in the shadow of the reality that is ours.

Let us take the case of Abraham. He lived in the Bronze Age, about five hundred years before the Ten Commandments were revealed. Therefore, neither his morality nor that of the other patriarchs can be judged by the Commandments. Considering that he lived around 1900 B.C., his faith and personal walk with God are a marvel. Scripture does not condemn the patriarchs Joseph and Moses for marrying foreign wives either, for God dealt with the issue of foreign wives after the Exile, some seven hundred years later.

Polygamy was tolerated among the kings long after it was forbidden to the people. Probably the people did not want their kings to be different from those of other nations. However, since both David and Solomon are two of the Bible's heroes, we must also look at the slowness of obedience to God's perfect will here. We cannot judge them by Christian standards, however, for they did not have the light of Christ.

The cries for revenge in the Psalter often come from the most ancient psalms, from the time before the knowledge about eternal life was given. People at that time demanded that justice be done here in this life, so that death could be faced in peace. Their cries for justice, coming from deep pain, are still echoed by those who suffer unjustly today. One would hope that today's sufferers would use these psalms with Christian love, for Jesus asked that all judgment be left to God. When we pray the prayers of the Old Testament, we want to see all issues through the eyes of our Savior. This does not lessen the prayers' value but enhances it.

ANCIENT SCRIBAL MISTAKES

Each text of Scripture was copied hundreds of times by scribes in order to make the sacred scrolls available to people everywhere. Would it not be a miracle if none of these scribes made any mistakes? Does the inspiration and inerrancy of the Bible preclude all human error down to the last jot and tittle?

The various manuscripts of the Bible were laboriously copied by hand for centuries before the age of printing. Of course mistakes occurred. A scribe was distracted and left a word out, or even a line. Or perhaps he wrote the same letter twice. If the text used an abbreviation for a word, the copyist might misunderstand it. Some teachers wrote notes in the margins, and some copyists felt that they had to copy these also!

Then there was the storage problem, which led to manuscripts being partially destroyed. Some of the text might disappear until more discoveries were made. Is this what happened to the short ending of the Gospel of Mark, for example? In most manuscripts the last chapter ends halfway through a sentence in verse 8. Later scribes tried to rectify the problem by inserting the missing verses.

The story of the adulteress is in the eighth chapter of John's Gospel, but it did not belong there originally. It is a genuine account of an incident in the life of Jesus, and fits very well in its present context to show Jesus as the merciful judge. But where was it originally? Some manuscripts put it in John 21 or even in Luke 21. A stray text that finally found a home!

These scribal errors do not need to disturb us, for there were thousands of copies of each text, and the correct reading was always retrievable. Scholars compare the various manuscripts in order to give us the very best rendering of each word, phrase, line, and paragraph. Whenever new manuscripts are discovered, they are examined minutely to see if they will throw more light on our existing texts. A good translation will note in the margin any obscure texts. It will also admit to the scholarly guesswork used to render the passage as intelligible as possible. The result of this process is a remarkable fidelity to the original manuscripts.

EIGHT

Archeology:
The Silent Witness

I F THE TRADITION OF BOTH Old Testament and New Testament believers is the vocal witness to the truth of the
Bible, archeology is the eloquent silent witness that offers a
window on the ancient world of the Middle East, allowing us
to share in the biblical story as told in the remnants that
have turned up in stone, clay tablets, pottery, parchment,
and other artifacts found everywhere there. Because the
facts celebrated in the Bible are based on actual historical
events, we would expect archeology to affirm or deny them.
In fact, archeology has proved to be a mine of information
surpassing expectation. It has thrown light on the peoples of
the Bible lands, their culture, and their religion.

The value of archeological finds lies in the fact that the
Bible does not ever set out to tell the whole story even of its
greatest heroes. Yet each one of these people lived in a
particular environment that somehow explains their way of
life and customs. Take Abraham, for instance. We can find
out from nonbiblical sources about the world that he lived
in, and so come to understand more deeply what he said and
did.

The Bible never gives a complete record of any event;

73

nonbiblical sources supplement this record and help complete the picture. For example, archeology has revealed that King Omri, dismissed by the Books of Kings in six verses (1 Kgs 16:23-28), was known to the Assyrians and was the conqueror of Moab. We discover that King Ahab sent an army against the Assyrians also. Neither of these facts, which would have been important politically, are mentioned in the Bible.

Archeology has provided information on ancient languages, enabling scholars to translate difficult passages of the Bible more accurately. Comparing words in similar languages has made it possible to read a datum that the translator had missed, giving important information of historical and geographic value. Archeology has also done a great deal to dismiss the arguments of the rationalists that biblical history was of doubtful worth. Scholars now admit that archeology has confirmed the overall historicity of the biblical tradition.

TESTIMONIES IN STONE

The stories of Creation and the Flood are not only told in Genesis, but also on clay tablets found in the library of Nineveh, the Assyrian capital. The differences lie in the monotheism of Israel and the polytheism of Assyria. That there were great flood(s) in Mesopotamia has been proved by the silt deposits in several excavated sites, such as Ur, where Abraham originated. Ancient lists of the kings of Mesopotamia speak of "before the flood" and "after the flood." These kings are given very long lives, as in Genesis 11.

Archeology has shown that Ur was an important town in Mesopotamia in 2000 B.C., the time of Abraham. Evidence has been found of the Amorites and the Hittites, two tribes mentioned frequently in these early narratives. From the many findings of all sorts—pottery, clay tablets, documents of commercial and political deals, and figurines in bronze, clay, wood, and camel bone—archeologists have been able to reconstruct life as it was in the time of the patriarchs (the Bronze Age).

Statuettes of the gods worshiped by these peoples; including the god Ba'al found at Tyre and dating back to 1400 B.C., shows that the Israelites were up against a well-established pagan religion. The prophets testify to the struggle of Israel to eliminate the Ba'als from the land. The household gods taken by Rachel (Gn 31:19) were normal for those times. Statues of golden calves have been found also, some of which are now in the British Museum.

The land of the Pharaohs has turned out to be the archeologist's paradise, for so many exciting finds have come from there up to very recently. The tombs of the Pharaohs have yielded much information regarding their civilization. Archeology has provided proof of many things in the Joseph story also, including the titles of offices given to people like Joseph and other high officials.

It may have been during the time of the Hyksos kings of Egypt that the family of Jacob was welcomed there (1700 B.C.). These kings were Semites like Jacob and his sons, and they had made their capital in the Goshen area, where Jacob's family settled. An Egyptian brick made of chopped straw and mud from the Nile, and bearing the name of Rameses II, dates from 1330 B.C., the time of the Exodus. Some archeologists believe they can trace the path of Israel through the wilderness and the conquering of the land. Finds along the way have thrown much light on these events.

Other finds that confirm Old Testament history are Solomon's stables at Megiddo and David's citadel in Jerusalem. The Siloam inscription, taken from the walls of King Hezekiah's tunnel, and the ruins of the palace of Ahab and Jezebel in Samaria are other pointers to historicity.

Very interesting indeed have been the excavations done in Assyria and Babylon, and much has been revealed that corroborates biblical records. For example, Susa (or Shushan), about two hundred miles east of Babylon, was the capital of the Persian kings, and it is here that the stories of Esther and King Ahasuerus and Daniel took place. The site covers four thousand nine hundred acres. Excavators discovered the "citadel of Susa," mentioned in Esther 1:5, including the harem, the throne room, many inner and outer courts, the palace gardens, stairways, terraces, and so on. The whole site confirms the accuracy of the Book of Esther, even to such detail as the description of the floor of the throne room and the adjoining gardens (Est 1:5-7). The famous stele of the code of Hammurabi was found there also, one of the most important legal documents from antiquity.

REMNANTS OF AN ANCIENT WORLD

Archeologists in Nineveh uncovered Sennacherib's royal palace, the approach to which was lined with the now-famous winged bulls. The palace was of immense dimensions, with slabs of sculptured alabaster telling the stories of the wars and exploits of the kings. They relate the kings' campaigns into Judea and the siege of Jerusalem, in which Hezekiah and Isaiah were involved.

This account both agrees with that of the Bible and supplements it. It says that Sennacherib "shut up Hezekiah like a caged bird," but it gives no reason for not capturing the city. Isaiah, chapters 36 to 37, and 2 Kings, chapters 18 and 19, tell us that God intervened on behalf of his people! Sennacherib's last days, described in 2 Kings 19:36-37, are confirmed on clay tablets found in Esarshaddon's palace south of Nineveh.

Ten miles north of Nineveh lies the capital of Sargon, King of Assyria. It was a twenty-five-acre palace in the city of

Khorsabad. Here again were miles of bas reliefs, pictures, and inscriptions on all the walls of the palace, enough to bewilder the scientists. The only biblical reference to this great king is given in Isaiah 20:1. Scholars for a long time had thought Isaiah wrong here, but now they can read Sargon's version of the capture of Samaria and his destruction of Ashdod.

About twenty miles south of Nineveh is the modern Nimrod, on the west bank of the Tigris River. Genesis 10:11 calls it by its ancient name of Calah and says that it was first built by Nimrod. Here were found the remains of the palaces of three kings of Assyria; Ashurbanipal (885-860 B.C.), Shalmanaser III (860-825 B.C.), and Esarshaddon (680-669 B.C.). Among the many wall sculptures found, there were the records of the victories of Tiglath-Pileser III, the Pul of 2 Kings 15:19. These sculptures appear to have been taken from an older palace and placed in the present one by Esarshaddon.

Archeologists also found a famous black marble obelisk in the central building of Shalmanaser. It depicts campaigns against both Hazael of Damascus and Jehu of Israel. One of the bas reliefs depicts Jehu, son of Omri, bowing to the ground and paying tribute in gold to King Shalmanaser. This is the only known sculptured relief of an Israelite king.

Many great names are associated with the city of Babylon which has been excavated also. Hammurabi (1728-1686 B.C.) may have built it. The city declined under Nebuchadnezzar II (604-562 B.C.), and fell to a lower state under Belshazzar. It finally came to ruin under the Parthians in 130 B.C.

Many of the city gates have been uncovered, the Isthar Gate being the most spectacular. It has 575 enamelled dragons, bulls, and lions. This was the entrance to the main processional street, which led past the royal palace to the temple of Marduk. The palace is gorgeously decorated, and the ruins of the celebrated "Tower of Babel" are there. It was known as "E-Temen-an-ki," which means the "House of the

Foundation Platform of Heaven and Earth." This illuminates the biblical story of the Tower of Babel.

Evidence of the famous Hanging Gardens of Babylon, one of the wonders of the ancient world, was found too in these ruins. Almost three hundred tablets were discovered, relating to ordinary life between 595 and 570 B.C. One clay tablet describes the capture of Jerusalem on March 16, 597 B.C., by Nebuchadnezzar. It tells us that Joiachin, the king of Judah, and his five young sons were held captive in Babylon, and that Zedekiah was appointed king in place of Joiachin.

NEW TESTAMENT SITES

Pilgrims to Palestine today can see for themselves how archeology has proven the factual basis of the events related in the New Testament. All the sites relevant to Jesus' life and ministry have been uncovered. The New Testament Jericho, which is two miles southwest of the Old Testament city of the same name, has been uncovered. It was the winter resort of the Herods, and very elaborately designed for the pleasure of their guests. The site commemorating Jesus' baptism has been identified as Bethabara, and this is mentioned in some of the manuscripts of John's Gospel (1:28). This very ancient site is the Beth-Arabah of Joshua 15:6.

Bethlehem is sacred to both the Old Testament and the New Testament. It is the city of David, and the place where he was anointed king. Here Rachel is buried, and one can visit the field of Boaz where Ruth gleaned. There are also the shepherds' fields of Luke 2. The church of the nativity was built by Constantine in A.D. 326 over a cave that had long been venerated as the birthplace of Jesus. Jerome said that in A.D. 135 the Romans, obviously trying to destroy Christianity, had a pagan shrine inserted into this cave for some time.

RECORDS, LETTERS, AND OTHER WRITINGS

Extreme nineteenth-century critics like Baur and those of the Tubingen School in Germany claimed that Luke's descriptions in Acts were not historically accurate. Yet extensive archeological research has demonstrated that the double work, Luke-Acts, was accurate and reflected a thorough knowledge of the first century A.D.

One point of continued argument is the time of the census mentioned in Luke 2:2 and Acts 5:38. Archeology has come to our aid again here, although the matter is not completely settled. Luke says that the census that took Mary and Joseph to Bethlehem took place when Quirinius was governor of Syria. The sons of Herod were ruling Palestine at the time, and Pontius Pilate was governor of Judea. Annas and Caiaphas were the high priests.

All of this can be checked from public records and writings of the time. Herod the Great reigned from 37 to 4 B.C. During this time Caesar Augustus ordered a census "of the whole world," which of course refers to those provinces under Roman rule. This census, which was taken for taxation purposes, involved the mass movement of people to their hometowns. It had to be done in stages for fear of uprisings. Augustus wanted a systematic enrollment of the Roman Empire, which would take some time and also some organization. Documentary evidence from Egypt shows that fourteen years lapsed between enrollments and that these enrollments were carried out by household. These findings show actual census papers for enrollments in Egypt for the years A.D. 90, 104, 118, 132, and so on until A.D. 230.

It seems from all the evidence available that Jesus was born in 7 or 6 B.C. The census cycle gives a similar date. The historian Josephus speaks of a Quirinius as governor of Syria in A.D. 6, but he is not considered to be completely reliable on this point. Perhaps there were two people of that name, which is not beyond the realm of possibility. An inscription at Antioch of Pisidia refers to Quirinius ruling from 8 to 6 B.C., the time of Jesus' birth.

Luke speaks of a famine in Acts 11:27-30, and this is well attested. Roman records speak of famine prices under Claudius, resulting from bad harvests. An inscription points to a famine in Asia Minor. Paul made a collection for the poor Christians in Jerusalem during this time. Archeologists have followed Paul's missionary journeys and agreed with the Acts account of them.

Recent findings from Chenoboskion in Egypt have uncovered a Gnostic library of no small significance for scholars. Up to now the only references to Gnosticism were in the writings of the church fathers. Now we have forty of the original treatises, which throw light both on the works of the early church fathers and on John's Gospel. For some time critics claimed that John was influenced by the Gnostics. Now it is clear that he was not. The treatises show the Gnostics to be outrageously heretical, whereas John reveals the purity of God's Word in a most sublime fashion. The Dead Sea Scrolls are in line with John's thought but he was not in any way dependent on them. They simply agree that there are two principles at work in the world, one good and one evil.

A veritable mine of papyri has been uncovered in the past one hundred years, especially in Egypt. Those writings shed much light on the life and times of the people, and also include many valuable fragments of both the Old and New Testaments. A great variety of letters, both personal and official, have been found, allowing us to "hear" these first century people communicate with each other.

Many of these documents enlighten us on the use of words in the New Testament. For example *an arrabon* (Greek) was an "earnest," an advance payment in expectation of full payment later. In one of the letters a woman had sold a cow, and received one thousand drachmae as an earnest. The word is used by Paul with this exact meaning in

2 Corinthians 1:22; 5:5; and Ephesians 1:14.

An inscription of an ossuary in Jerusalem throws light on the use of the word *corban* in the synoptics (Mk 7:9-13). It reads, "All that a person may find of profit in this ossuary is corban to God from the one who lies within it." Everything was dedicated to God, and not to be used by anyone.

Part III

The Problem of Understanding

NINE

Can We Really Understand the Bible?

A NYONE WHO HAS STUDIED SHAKESPEARE knows that the meaning of literary works is not always immediately obvious. Students struggle with words and phrases that were common to Shakespeare's first audience but are not so in a different country, culture, and time. So it is with all great works of literature, including the Bible.

Exegesis is the science whereby scholars determine the correct interpretation of a text. The Bible is unique, for it is the Word of God coming to us in the words of men. Therefore, biblical exegesis demands that we find out what both the human author and the Holy Spirit are trying to say. And to complicate matters even further, it is always possible that the divine author wanted to say more than the human author could express.

Because the Bible is expressed in human words, it is subject to examination like all other literature. But because it is also the Word of God, it contains a depth of meaning that mere literary examination will not uncover. Hence we need interpreters or exegetes. Some of the most famous of these were the early church fathers, like Origen, Jerome, and Augustine. From a later age came the Jewish Masorettes,

Albert the Great, and Thomas Aquinas, just to name a few whose scholarship has had lasting effects on the life of the church. The works of these and other exegetes are still available.

The scholarship of the early church fathers was matched only by their holiness. Hence they speak to us with authority even today. They are also unique in that they are the link between us and the Apostles.

This does not belittle the work of scholars and exegetes today, who are doing trojan work on our behalf. To accomplish their task they have to be fluent in the biblical languages and in the history and geography of the ancient Near East. They must master archeology, paleontology, anthropology, oriental psychology, and many other specialized sciences. They study all the literature of the cultures surrounding Palestine in biblical times. All this is to bring us a deeper understanding of the thinking and practices of a people who have so profoundly affected our life.

THE CLOUD OF WITNESSES

Over and above these human sciences, the Christian exegete must take account of the fact that the Bible was given to us, in both of its Testaments, by a living tradition. The literature side of it can be studied with the tools of literary analysis, but the revelatory aspect can be interpreted only by the believers who passed it on to us. That means that the Jewish community of the Old Testament and the Jewish community today are the authority on the Old Testament as the Hebrew Scriptures. The church is the final authority on the New Testament. It is also an authority on the Old Testament, since the Christian community inherited the Hebrew Scriptures and therefore has the right to interpret them according to the light of Christ. Also, the earliest Christians were Jews, and the learned among them, like Paul, could interpret the Jewish Scriptures authoritatively.

The Bible, therefore, is the unique and inimitable crystallization of the faith of the people of God. The biblical authors are the witnesses raised up by God to pass this testimony on to us, which they did under the influence of the Holy Spirit. The Holy Spirit continues to work through the witnesses he raises up in every age to interpret what he is saying to the churches. He uses scholars and the church's magisterium. He also uses the saints and mystics of every age, people who may not be scholars in the technical sense but who are very much in touch with the Lord through a life of holiness. Therefore the living tradition continues throughout the life of the church, and the Lord constantly speaks through a great cloud of witnesses (Heb 12:1).

Modern witnesses do not speak in isolation but as part of a church governed by the pope, the bishops, and the magisterium. These men, in their role as shepherds of the flock of God, have the task of discerning the true prophet from the false. Decisions, even of this body, are not made in isolation from the long history of the church or without reference to the apostolic fathers. Each of us is under authority, so that the Holy Spirit can guide the people of God.

To this end it is important to say that there is no such thing as a "Catholic" or "Protestant" interpretation of Scripture, for such terms were unknown to the authors of either testament. We can only speak of a correct or incorrect interpretation, or say that a writer has gone away from the intention of the biblical author. Great scholars from all the Christian denominations work closely together to try to bring us correct exegesis. They also work with Jewish scholars concerning the Old Testament.

OPINION VERSUS TRUTH

There is a lingering fear among Catholics with regard to private interpretation, although many of us do not understand the term. Sometimes this fear shows itself as a refusal to use our minds on the texts, even of the New Testament, lest we "get it wrong." Some people even give up trying to understand the Bible, and this is a great loss.

A private interpretation that "reads" a different message than was intended by either of the two authors has to be wrong. This process of "reading into" the text what is not there is called eisegesis, and it does not bring forth the Word of God. Exegesis is the process whereby we get from a text what the Holy Spirit put into it in the first place.

It would be very dangerous to teach *as Scripture* what is, in fact, one's own opinion. All responsible teachers alert their audiences when they are giving a personal opinion on a subject. Paul's anathema against teaching another gospel must be remembered (Gal 1:6-8). No matter who we are, pope or pauper, we are permitted to teach only what the Holy Spirit has revealed. Responsible teachers take into account the teaching of the church and the findings of scholars to assist them in their onerous task of transmitting the Word of God faithfully.

For instance, the Gospels reveal that Jesus of Nazareth is both God and Man, that he had an earthly mother but no earthly father, that his mother was a virgin, that he was crucified, died, and then rose from the dead. We cannot teach otherwise. The interpreter's work is to illuminate difficult phrases and explain what the authors intended to say. This involves translation across cultures in the interests of clarification. The interpreter does not have the task of imparting new revelation!

The church exercises her office as official interpreter of the Scriptures only when scholars or teachers go wrong. Otherwise she leaves them scope for research. The works of individuals in the church do not come under the heading of "private" interpretation. All works, even of renowned scholars, are simply the work of individuals who put their scholarship and their faith at the service of Christendom. They add their voices to the sea of witnesses raised up by God.

None of these works is infallible. They form part of an ever-growing stream in the effort to experience the fullness of the promise of Jesus in John 14:26: "The Paraclete, the Holy Spirit, whom the Father will send in my name, will teach you everything and remind you of all I have said to you."

PRIVATE READING

Millions of people read the Scriptures every day for private devotion. They expect the Holy Spirit to speak to them personally through the text at hand. Sometimes they will receive a message from the Lord that the human author never thought of specifically. This is not private interpretation but listening to the Lord, who continues to speak to his children for their salvation. Those who do Scripture study alongside their reading and meditation receive insights into the Word of God, both for themselves and others. The saints and mystics fit this category, as do millions of so-called "ordinary" Christians.

One abuse that we must be aware of is a practice called "cutting" the texts. This approach borders on superstition. The Bible falls open, and whatever text catches the eye is said to be the Holy Spirit speaking. We may hear the Lord speaking to us in this way, but we need to prayerfully discern this. We have a necessary warning in the example of a person opening to the text, "Judas went out and hung himself." Not happy with this, the person tries again, only to read: "Go thou and do likewise!" Readers need to be aware too that words in the text may not have the same meaning as in the English dictionary, for the Bible uses words according to the thinking of the authors.

THE MODE AND THE MESSAGE

If we are to understand the Bible as literature, it is necessary to look at the literary modes or forms used by the authors. The "Dogmatic Constitution on Divine Revelation" (Vat II, ch 3.12) says that "in determining the intention of the sacred writers, attention must be paid, *inter alia*, to 'literary forms, for the fact is that truth is differently presented and expressed in the various types of historical writing, in prophetical and poetical texts' and in other forms of literary expression. Hence the exegete must look for that meaning, which the sacred writer, in a determined situation and given the circumstances of his time and culture, intended to express and did in fact express, through the medium of a literary form. Rightly to understand what the sacred author wanted to affirm in his work, due attention must be paid both to the customary and characteristic patterns of perception, speech and narrative which prevailed at the age of the sacred writer, and to the conventions which the people of his time followed in their dealings with one another."

In our everyday lives we too use different literary forms. A letter to a friend is a very different type of communication than our income tax returns! When reading a newspaper we recognize the difference between the historical account, the scandal story, the editorial comment, and the football results, and we evaluate the information accordingly. We also discriminate between a magazine article and an historical novel. We make use of an amazing number of literary forms every day!

When we come to read the Bible we are faced with exactly the same phenomenon, for the sacred authors employed many forms of communication in transmitting revelation. To find out what an author really intended, and to eliminate what he did not intend, one must determine the literary mode that he used. We would not expect a poet to express historical facts in the same way as the historian. Neither should we expect the ancient storytellers, who had to teach as well as entertain their audiences, to teach history like twentieth-century scientists.

Some of the literary modes of the Bible are obvious. The Psalms are a collection of poems, hymns, and songs of praise. When reading them, we take poetic license into account. The poet might ask the planets to join us in praising God! The Psalms often personify death too. The "second death," being banished from God's presence after one's physical death, is sometimes called "the pit," as distinct from the grave (Ps 69:15).

I will deal with more literary modes in chapter 10. It suffices here to say that we must keep the author's mode in mind when we are trying to discern his message.

LETTERS FROM MISSIONARIES

The Apostles and evangelists were intent on taking the Christian message to the ends of the earth. They were not historians, although all that they taught was based on history. They were a combination of pastors, evangelists, and theologians who sought the conversion of their listeners (Jn 20:30-31). The material was adjusted, therefore, to suit the intention of the speaker or writer.

None of the evangelists set out to give us a biography of Jesus. They kept to the story of salvation and mentioned the things that happened through Jesus because he was the Savior. If we try to force them to become historians when that was not their intention, then we do violence to their work.

Most of the New Testament books are, in fact, letters sent to a church to answer local problems. When we read them we must bear in mind that we are hearing only one side of a story. Scholars try to piece together the debate for us so that we can read the letters with more understanding.

Sometimes Paul gets upset and indulges in polemics and exaggerated speech in dealing with his opponents. For example, he tells the people who insist on circumcision to castrate themselves (Gal 5:12; Phil 3:2-3)! Here we have a worried missionary who cannot bear the thought of his converts going back on their commitment to Christ. He expresses himself passionately, in language that would not be acceptable today. But he must be understood according to his own times.

Paul does not really want his opponents to castrate themselves, any more than Jesus wants us to cut out our eyes or cut off our hands when they are the agents of sin (Mt 18:8-9). Jesus speaks of the eye and the hand as symbols of all that we crave and all that we do. He is making the point that if anything that we want or do leads us away from God, then we must cut it out! This is a radical call to repentance and self-discipline.

JONAH TEACHES A LESSON

The Book of Jonah is a satire on the prevailing attitudes of Israel towards the Gentiles in the century just prior to the coming of Christ. It's a wonderful and amusing tale, and its lessons are deep and penetrating. It forms a theological treatise whose doctrines mark one of the peaks of the Old Testament.

There was a real prophet Jonah in the northern kingdom at the time of Jeroboam II (2 Kgs 14:25). The main character of the Book of Jonah, however, is presented as a caricature of a prophet. In fact, everyone in the story is likeable except him! The Lord is the hero of the story. He accomplishes his will despite the disobedience and stubbornness of his messenger.

This book was written when the great era of prophecy was over, and there were no great leaders in the land. The author wants his people to see that God can accomplish things by using anyone, even a reluctant messenger. This lesson prepares us for the fact that Jesus was about to appear on the stage of history to ask reluctant Israel to go and preach to the Gentiles, and what a struggle they had to obey! History has shown that the Lord succeeded in his mission to convert the Gentiles, just as the author of Jonah had predicted.

The universalist approach to salvation in Jonah was a correction to the separatist and exclusivist policies of the time of Ezra and Nehemiah. God is presented as the Savior and Lord of all peoples who can even convert their greatest enemy, the king of Nineveh (there are no historical records of such an event, however). This book, with its emphasis on the mercy of God for all sinners and his love for the Gentiles as well as the Jews, brings us to the very threshold of the New Testament. Jesus quoted the book twice: He compared Jonah's stay in the fish of his own three days in the grave (Mt 12:14), and he cited the Ninevites as an example of conversion (Mt 12:41). Jesus' references to this book in no way deems it historical. Jesus could quote from this story in the same way that we quote parables to make a point.

TEN

A Wealth
of Literature

Biblical authors, like all other authors, used many different ways to communicate their message. The Bible abounds in legal codes, genealogies, personal testimony, and long speeches. Forms that require more explanation for their use in the Bible are the legendary epic, Midrash or inspired commentaries, apocalyptic writings, parables, and proverbs. Once we are alerted to these different literary forms of communication, we read them with more confidence and understanding.

THE GREAT HEROES

Every nation and culture boasts of its epic heroes, wonderful leaders of a glorious past who embody the history, culture, and aspirations of the people. The older the story, the more likely it is to fall into this category, since all ancient history was kept alive by oral tradition.

The basics of the story are historical, but as teachers related these facts to a new generation, they interpreted, illustrated, and explained, so the story "grew" with time. If the events recounted had to do with major national happenings, then the story tended to be dramatized to make it "hear" well. All biblical epics are based on real heroes and real facts, such as the Exodus under Moses, the conquering of the Promised Land under Joshua, and the events pertaining to the great patriarchs.

The rhythmic style and wonderful imagery of the epic narrative give it the sound of poetry. As we read the story of the crossing of the Red Sea, for example, we can see the helpless slaves trapped between the sea and Pharaoh's army. Their great hero, Moses, prays to God, the Savior and defender of the poor and needy. The sea opens (for God the Creator can do anything), and the people march triumphantly to freedom "with walls of water to the right and left of them."

When the last Israelite is saved, the sea just as dramatically closes. God himself, the just judge, drowns Pharaoh's army. The wicked king is vanquished by a foe whom he cannot see and in whom he refuses to believe (Ex 14:15-31).

The power of this story is immense, as is its emotional appeal. It glorifies both God and Moses. Its purpose is to teach about God and his goodness. He is merciful to those who follow his ways, but those who remain obdurate, as the Pharaoh did, must face the consequences of their actions. The Egyptians could have experienced God as Savior, as Israel did, but Pharaoh's stubborn refusals of grace forced God to show his hand as just judge instead. The story tells the poor and helpless of the world that God is their champion. He is the one who will take up their cause, defend them, and make them his own people. When God acts, no power on earth can stop him.

The crossing of the Red Sea was a great moment of deliverance, and from it Israel and Christianity have derived much instruction and inspiration. We all have these salvific moments in our lives, and it is important to value them and tell others of them. Thus our own "epic saga" can be a rich story of God's faithfulness and mercy.

INSPIRED COMMENTARIES

The Bible is unique in offering us not only text but also commentary on many points. These commentaries are part of the inspired Word of God; the Holy Spirit wanted them given to us. He also wanted to show us how to meditate on the Word of God.

These commentaries in Scripture are very different from the critical studies done by scholars today. They are more like the spiritual commentaries of saints and holy people, who share with us the richness of God's Word. Midrash, for example, is a type of exegesis that priests and ministers still use when preparing a talk or homily. It was one of the most popular ways to reflect on Scripture in the Old Testament. During the time of the Exile the people were deprived of both temple and synagogue, so the memory of the texts and the commentaries of their saints became very important. After the Exile Midrash was studied in the rabbinic schools.

There were two main types of Midrash. The *halakah* consisted of explanations of the law, deriving principles of conduct from it. The *haggadah* is an explanation of the narrative passages of the Pentateuch, deriving lessons from it. Both types of commentary came from meditation on the text, and the purpose was the practical application to daily life.

Chapters 10 through 19 of the Book of Wisdom form a commentary on the great salvific events of Israel's history. Midrash is also found in the New Testament, though scholars differ as to how much of it is this type of writing. A good example is Paul's allusions to Abraham. In Romans 4 Paul sets forth Abraham as our model of faith. In Galatians 4 he sees Abraham's two wives as symbols of the two Covenants God has made—first with Israel, then with the church. Hebrews uses Midrash in chapter 11 to set forth the heroes of the faith.

HOPE FOR HARD TIMES

The apocalyptic writings were widely diffused in Israel from 200 B.C. to A.D. 100. The nation was groaning under foreign oppression once again. Alexander the Great brought the Persian Empire to an end in 331 B.C., but he died without an heir in 323 B.C. His army generals divided his empire among themselves; and a period of struggle among the new dynasties ensued. Israel was caught between the Ptolemies in Egypt and the Seleucids who controlled Syria and Palestine. In the Books of the Maccabees we read that the Jews revolted against the infamous Antiochus IV Epiphanes, who had desecrated the temple, forced the people to eat unclean foods, and finally outlawed their faith.

It was during these struggles that the Book of Daniel came into being, even though it is set in the context of the Babylonian exile. Its author chose to remain anonymous, and like the author of Jonah, chose an ancient hero as his main character. Danel (not Daniel) is mentioned in Ezekiel 14:14-20 as an ancient sage whose wisdom was well known. The book is somewhat ineptly called a prophetic book, because it actually contains several types of literature. It is broadly divided into three sections, each with different literary forms: (1) the adventures of Daniel and his companions in chapters 1 through 6; (2) apocalyptic revelations in chapters 7 through 12; (3) additions in chapters 13 and 14.

The story of Daniel and his companions is probably best classified as Haggidic Midrash. The kernel of the tale was already in use. The author decided to apply it to the situation of his own time, but cloaked it with historical details of olden days (none of them too accurate) to protect his message during the persecution of Epiphanes. It is typical of apocalyptic literature that the author hides his message from the undiscerning reader.

Daniel and his companions are being persecuted by a foreign king, who does not understand that they worship the one true God. Neither threats of death nor the promise of rewards shift them from their steadfast faith in God. The Jews of 167 B.C. would have identified with Daniel's situation, for it reflected exactly their own dilemma (see 1-2 Mcs). A key point is when Daniel says that even if God does not deliver them from the power of the wicked king, they will remain faithful (Dn 3:18-19). God does deliver his servants, a wonder that makes the evil king acknowledge the true God.

The second section, the apocalyptic revelation, concerns God's secret message to his faithful servants. This message is intended to build their faith and trust in God as the Lord of history and the ultimate ruler of the universe. The author represents the four great world empires as four beasts, whose plans and politics oppose God's plans for his people. Much attention is given to the fourth beast, which represents the Greeks, the power the Jews were struggling with at the time. God is presented as the judge who will punish speedily. God is about to send the mysterious Son of Man to establish the messianic kingdom. Considering that this work was written around 167 B.C., this is a very accurate prediction indeed!

The setting of apocalyptic writing during a time of persecution means that the author considers what is happening in the light of God's ultimate purpose for the world. It is a message of hope in God's ultimate triumph, the establishment of his Kingdom. All ages—past, present, and future—are seen in this light and therefore are prophetic of the final outcome. The author sees a prophetic dimension to all history, during which God reveals his secrets to chosen messengers who can give both hope and light to others. Here we see the importance of looking for God's action in our own time.

There are other examples of apocalyptic writings in the Old Testament, in parts of Ezekiel, Zechariah, and Joel. The Book of Revelation is the only example in the New Testament (apart from three eschatological discourses in the synoptic Gospels). Here too in Revelation, the Christian community is under persecution, and John hides his message with symbols understood by his audience.

John's vision is different from those in the Old Testament because the Messiah has come, and the secret seals of God are now opened by him, unraveling the destiny of individuals and nations. Like other apocalyptic writings, it speaks of a confrontation between God and world powers, with the victory, as ever, going to God. John brings us a vision of Heaven itself. He shows us the glory of the saints in God's presence and the ultimate victory of the Lamb and his bride. All the poor and helpless of the world who have turned to God find help and salvation.

PROVERBS AND PARABLES

These are a type of communication known to every culture and every age. People use both proverbs and parables so easily that they are hardly aware of it.

Proverbs are pithy sayings that are true to life. Here are some Irish examples: "The only cure for love is marriage"; "There is no strength without unity"; "The mouth of the grave often feeds the mouth of the poor." Israel's collection of proverbs covers every aspect of life, from moral behavior in private and public affairs, to how to raise a family, run a business, and succeed.

Parables, on the other hand, are fictional stories told to teach a lesson. The literary form is didactic fiction. The parable uses everyday life to teach the lessons of life, but the story is always presented in fictional form so that the concentration is on the lesson to be learned. Preachers do this all the time when they tell stories that illustrate their point in a sermon.

This definition of parable may disturb some of us who have felt that the prodigal son in Luke was a real person. The answer to that is, he is a real person. Is he you? The Bible has presented many people who would fit the role of the prodigal son—one who sins greatly and then repents. Two that come to mind readily are David in the Old Testament and Peter and Mary Magdalen in the New Testament. This does not mean that the story is about them. It just fits their case, for each of them discovered the unfathomable love of God through their experience of repentance. The story is broadened to fit anyone in these circumstances.

The advantage of a parable is that it is a story. It captures the imagination, even if one is not ready to learn its lesson. But since the story will be easily remembered, one can inquire later regarding its meaning. It is a way of giving us time to deal with life and its needs, and of leaving the invitation of grace with us until we are ready to turn to the Lord.

The parable is also useful when presenting an unpalatable truth. The reasoning of the story can be seen, and this helps us to deal with the challenge presented. For example, the elder brother in the story of the prodigal son is an unwelcome presentation of the sins of good people. It illustrates how we can be apparently close to God but very far from his way of thinking or from his love. In fact, one can be lost in legalism, bigotry, and unforgiveness, while the doctor of our souls waits patiently for us to come for help. The pleading of the father with this son is the most sad moment in the whole tale, for it is the plea of God to good people to really become good, to allow his love to reign in their hearts. This parable ends with a plea for real holiness, and likeness to him who is love (1 Jn 4:16).

ELEVEN

The Bible Speaks on Different Levels

T HE PAPAL ENCYCLICAL *Divino Afflante Spiritu* is regarded among many as the *magna charta* for Catholic biblical scholars. In it Pope Pius XII urged all interpreters of Scripture to bear in mind that their greatest task is to determine and clearly define the literal sense of Scripture (section 2, paragraph 28), that is, the meaning the author intended to convey through his words. This literal sense is not always obvious to the reader, for some passages can be obscure. We need the help of scholars to unravel the text for us.

LITERALLY TRUE

What, for example, is the literal meaning of John 15, which speaks of Jesus as the vine, or John 10 which says that he is a good shepherd? What do the Psalms mean when they call God our rock or urge us to hide under the "shadow of his wings"? What did Jesus mean by saying that we must forgive seventy times seven times?

The answers are found by looking to what the authors

were trying to say to us. John was using favorite imagery for the people of God (see Is 5) when he compared Jesus and the church to a vine and its branches. John could transmit a lot of information through this image, for it reveals the intimacy between Jesus and his disciples in every age.

Likewise, John 10 is a parable based on Ezekiel 34, which refers to the leaders of Israel as shepherds. John wants to apply that teaching to the church. All the great shepherd leaders of the Old Testament prepared the way for *the shepherd* of God's people, namely Jesus, who is the only gate into the Kingdom of God.

When Jesus tells us to forgive seventy times seven times, we are not expected to do our arithmetic and say that it is impossible to forgive 490 times! Many feel that to forgive at all is impossible without the grace of God. The Gospel is speaking metaphorically here, telling us to live a life of forgiveness in imitation of Jesus. It is a call to the radical Christian life.

The Psalms, too, speak metaphorically when comparing God to a rock. The psalmists saw rock as material that never wore out, so it was an image of eternity. God is our eternal security.

Neither does the psalmist seek the "shadow of his wings" because God is thought of as a great bird. The Holy of Holies had the cherubim over the ark of the covenant protecting the glory of God. To come under the shadow of God's wings was a request for intimacy with him. However, Deuteronomy 32, which also speaks of God as our rock, compares him in verse 11 with the great eagle that carries its young and protects them with its outstretched wings. Here again the writer speaks of protection and intimacy and special relationship with God.

Notice that one needs to compare Scripture with Scripture to find other usages and thus discern the meaning of a phrase that may be strange to us. A good maxim for the interpreter is that "Scripture explains Scripture." If we interpret the author's words literally in every case, then we are in serious trouble. Jesus is not a vine, nor was he ever a shepherd. We are not to cut off our hands when we sin, and so on. Literalism, therefore, is wrong. What the author intended to say, using whatever form of speech or writing he chose, is the correct way to read him. The literary sense of a Gospel passage is the meaning that the evangelist gave to the words, whether he was quoting Jesus or not.

This literary sense of Scripture has taken on renewed importance for scholars today, who maintain that the literary sense of a text should be found before seeking any other meaning for it. In other words, we must determine what the author was saying to *his own immediate audience* before looking for any deeper or more extensive meaning in the text.

The church's struggles in the first century would have been uppermost in Mark's mind when he wrote his Gospel. The church in Rome was undergoing persecution. Historical records admit that while many died martyrs, others purchased their freedom by betrayal. Both Peter and Paul died as a result of such betrayals.

This could explain why Mark related the denials of Peter with such detail, including his running away in the garden and his cursing and swearing that he did not know Jesus. Mark could be using the incident of "Peter back there" to try to strengthen those tempted to deny the Lord now.

Mark has good news for the Christians under persecution: Jesus understood that the "spirit is willing, but the flesh is weak." He forgave Peter, and he would forgive them. He wants the present disciples in the church to recover and serve him faithfully unto death, as Peter has done in the present crisis. Following the same line of reasoning, Mark's account of what happened to Judas would stand as a sound warning to anyone tempted to go down that road.

THE SPIRIT'S HAND

Scripture comes from two hands, one of which is divine. This means that the literary sense is not the only way to read the text. Many times the Holy Spirit inspired authors to express things in ways that surpassed their own understanding, and later generations perceived this deeper meaning. This makes Scripture study very exciting. The "Dogmatic Constitution on Divine Revelation" (Vat II, ch 3.12) says: "But since sacred Scripture must be read and interpreted with its divine authorship in mind, no less attention must be devoted to the content and unity of the whole of Scripture, taking into account the tradition of the entire church and the analogy of faith, if we are to derive their true meaning from the sacred texts."

Each book of the Bible was composed separately, some of them over a long period of time. The Holy Spirit was very active at this stage of their development. Later, under the direction of the same Spirit, these books were collected and put into thematical order. This was done deliberately, and forever after each book would be found not only in the Bible but in that place, to be read in relation to the books around it. We have already illustrated this with regard to the Pentateuch, where we ended up with a five-part work with a continuous theme. The history books of Joshua and Kings followed, and the reader now listens to God dealing with a people over the centuries. We can detect the development of doctrine and the understanding of God's ways. The teachers, like the prophets and sages, quoted each other. By comparing their works we can more easily understand what was being said.

The same holds true for the New Testament. Each of the Gospels had its own separate history of development in the area that produced it. Later it found its way into the official church collection of sacred books. It was put into a particular order thematically, and this construction affected how we see its contents. Why, for example, did they put Matthew first, then Mark, Luke, and finally John? Why did they separate the Gospel of Luke from the Acts of the Apostles? Luke must have had them as one.

Reading the New Testament books in their present order shows progression in theme from the ministry of Jesus to the preaching of the Apostles, the founding of the church, its missionary growth, its first persecutions, and its internal struggles in Acts and the Epistles. Then comes its apocalyptic ending to round it all off.

Thus a unity was created both in the Old Testament and the New Testament, and just as importantly, *between* the Old Testament and New Testament. This unity between the testaments is important for interpretation, because the message of one set of books is colored by the other. The Old Testament is the preparation for the New Testament, and the New Testament is the fulfillment of the Old Testament. The Christian will see more in some Old Testament texts than was possible by looking at those texts in isolation (Lk 2:27, 44). Hindsight is the best sight for most of us, even when it comes to the saving events of history. We can see that the Holy Spirit had a hand in the arrangement of the texts, for if they had been left separated they would be a less powerful message than they are together.

THE OLD FORETELLS THE NEW

The spiritual interpretation of Scripture is as old as Scripture itself. It has influenced believers' lives more than the literal sense has. It is often called the typical sense, the spiritual sense, or the mystical sense. It is based on the fact that God ordered history in such a way that persons and events of one age could prefigure persons and events of a much later era.

Pope Pius XII highlighted this type of exegesis in *Divino*

Afflante Spiritu, (section 2, paragraphs 31-33). He said that what was said and done in the Old Testament was ordained and disposed by God with such extraordinary wisdom that things in the past prefigure in a spiritual way those that were to come under the dispensation of grace. This type of exegesis stresses the consistency of God's redemptive work and the progressive nature of revelation. Here the New Testament throws light on the Old Testament, and the Old Testament prepares for and explains the extraordinary events of the New Testament.

Let us look at an example. The story of Abraham's willingness to sacrifice Isaac has its own meaning in its context in Genesis. However, over and above that, Christians see Abraham as a type of God the Father, Isaac as a type of Jesus the Son, and the sacrifice of Isaac as prefiguring Calvary. John 19:17 alludes to this: Jesus set out for the hill of Calvary carrying the wood of the cross on his back, just as Isaac carried the wood for the sacrifice in the type. The obedience and surrender of Isaac to his father point to that of Jesus the beloved Son, just as the Crucifixion and Resurrection of Jesus are prefigured in the binding and unbinding of Isaac. Once the type has been discovered, then that text (here Gn 22) takes on an altogether new look, intended by the Holy Spirit but not seen by the human author "back there" in ancient history.

There are examples of this type of exegesis in the scriptural books themselves, thus lending weight to spiritual exegesis. Wisdom 11 through 19, for instance, reads the Exodus theme from the sacred scrolls and translates them into deliverance themes for the author's own day. Isaiah 40 to 66 uses the Exodus themes to speak of the return from Exile as a second exodus, with God himself as the liberator. Thus, the Exodus is an historical event, but its meaning can help future generations reach out to God in their need and allow him to be their liberator also. This understanding is based on the fact that God does not change and neither, unfortunately, does human nature nor our need for God's deliverance. God needs only to reveal his deliverance once, but all peoples may benefit from it, as all are his children. With the New Testament records of salvation, we can see the Exodus theme in an even more universalist way than either Wisdom or Deutero-Isaiah were able to do.

In the two centuries before Christ, Israel came to see the prophets in a new light. She had the complete collection of their works by then, and she also had the new work of Daniel with its apocalyptic content. At an earlier stage the Jews thought that the prophets had spoken only for their own day, but now they began to realize that there was also a futuristic dimension to prophecy.

Daniel's ability to express themes in a more general way helped the Jews apply prophecy more widely. Seeing each book in relation to the others in the Bible, Israel realized that God had given her many consistent messages regarding the Messiah, for example. The result was that she began to look in earnest for the Coming One, the Son of Man, the Suffering Servant of Isaiah. The expectation of the Messiah reached an all-time high just before the coming of Christ. The Holy Spirit had not only worked in the production of the Scriptures, but also in their compilation and in their interpretation.

THE NEW LOOKS AT THE OLD

The New Testament looked back at the Old Testament in this way also. Having the extra insight derived from the coming of Jesus and the redemption wrought by him, the church saw more in some Old Testament passages than was possible before the Christ event. Psalm 22 was seen to reflect with amazing accuracy the details of the passion of Jesus, and so the Gospels even quote it (Mt 27:46). The Servant Songs of Isaiah had the same function, and they also gave details of Jesus' miracle ministry. They influenced Mark's portrayal of Jesus as God's lowly servant. Isaiah 7:14 was now seen to foretell the virgin birth. The Exodus theme took on new dimensions: Christians saw that the Redemption wrought by Jesus, from spiritual slavery to spiritual freedom, had the elements of the Passover lamb, sacrifice, and covenant. This led to a new reading of Jeremiah 31:31-34, where the prophet speaks of the new covenant written on people's hearts. Jesus' miracle of the loaves was seen as the new manna miracle. In fact, Jesus was "read" by the evangelists as the new "Prophet like Moses," fulfilling Deuteronomy 18:15-18.

Paul and John use this type of interpretation. Paul uses the word *typos* in Romans 5:14, when he says that Adam is a type of Christ, and in 1 Corinthians 10:6, when he says that the things in the desert were types of things to come in the Redemption. The Exodus is a type of baptism in 1 Corinthians 10:2; the bronze serpent is a type of Christ's "lifting up" in John 3:14. The Paschal lamb is a type of Jesus as the victim in John 1:29. The type is always imperfect, a silhouette in the dim and distant past promising great things to come. The Holy Spirit used the New Testament authors to give us an inspired guide to reading the Old Testament. See, for example, Luke 24:27, 44.

TWELVE

An Age-Old Search for Meaning Becomes a Modern Battle

T HE EARLY CHURCH FATHERS continued the tradition of the New Testament in giving the spiritual exegesis of Scripture. Famous exegetes like Origen used allegory extensively to explain the Old Testament. Right up to modern times there is a long history of spiritual exegesis from all the monastic centers of Europe. Some wonderful classics like the works of John of the Cross, Meister Eckart, and Denis the Carthusian resulted from this. They are some of the treasures of the church.

The Protestant Reformation was a turning point, however, for the reformers reacted to a completely spiritual interpretation of the Bible. They insisted on the historical basis of the texts. Yet they remained firmly convinced, with the rest of Christendom, of the Christological reading of the Old Testament. Therefore many of them continued with a typological interpretation of the Old Testament. For Catholics, love for the church fathers meant that spiritual exegesis would never die, for the Fathers continued as the prime example of how to interpret Scripture.

The nineteenth and twentieth centuries heralded the critical exegesis of the Bible. Critical exegesis does not allow for typology or the spiritual interpretation, which is accepted among believers of all Christian churches. It sees the prophets as having very limited vision. It distinguishes clearly between the various stages of development of the New Testament; that is, between the theology of the New Testament books, which come from the first century A.D., and that of the later church. They see the Apostles as having very little understanding of Jesus before the Resurrection and even before Pentecost. They even say that Jesus did not proclaim himself Messiah during his lifetime.

THE FUNDAMENTALISTS RESPOND

There has been a strong reaction to more extreme liberal critical exegesis in the form of fundamentalism in the twentieth century. This was a felt need to hold on to the foundational teachings of the church in the face of the critics, who question even the virgin birth and the bodily resurrection of Jesus. Fundamentalism sees only one author in Scripture, namely, the Holy Spirit. The human authors are mere scribes who wrote down what they were given. We have now a battleground, with the fundamentalists on the one hand recognizing only the "God side" of Scripture and extreme liberal critics on the other seeing mostly the human side. This is a simplified view of a complex situation. We must watch out for the distortion and heresy that can result when either group takes its ideas too far.

The fundamentalists and extreme liberal critics also represent two sides of the debate on the Christ himself. One group sees him mostly as God, almost to the exclusion of his humanity. They are said to have a "high" Christology. The other side deals with him mostly as man, to such a degree that they ask whether he knew that he was God. No marks for guessing that this is "low" Christology!

It is significant that the discussion of Scripture and of Christ, who is also the Word of God, goes on together. Both Scripture and Christ have human and divine origins. When one takes away from the divinity of Christ, one also takes from the divine side of the Scriptures. The human authors are credited with no "special inspiration" from the Holy Spirit, so they do not foresee the Coming One. For example, Isaiah 7:14 is relegated to a prediction about the next king of Judah (Hezekiah, who was a good king but no Emmanuel!). This calls into question Matthew's quotation of this text to prove the virgin birth as foretold by the prophets, and on it goes with a domino effect that can be devastating.

The fundamentalist, on the other hand, claims that every word in the Old Testament speaks about Christ. According to them the prophets were speaking only of him, but in such a way that their lessons apply to similar situations anywhere. The fundamentalist ignores the prophet's concern for conditions of his own day. So the fundamentalist will go to great lengths to show the connections between passages, explain the typology, and apply biblical apocalyptic to today's events. In fact, fundamentalists very often read into Scripture things that the authors certainly did not think of.

Some fundamentalist groups also demand that first-century customs should be duplicated in the twentieth century, "for the Bible says so, and we are Bible believers." Twentieth-century women must have their heads covered and must not speak in church, for instance. Here they fail to distinguish revelation from human culture and custom, as if covering the head were an issue with God! Covering one's heart with repentance and love certainly is, as the New Testament clearly points out.

The "Dogmatic Constitution on Divine Revelation" (Vat II, ch 3.13) says: "Indeed the words of God, expressed in the words of men, are in every way like human language, just as the Word of the eternal Father, when he took on himself the flesh of human weakness, became like men." We who observe this debate, and who participate in it, can learn from both sides, while taking our faith from neither. We have a living tradition, oral as well as written, in our two-thousand-year-old church. We have the testimony of thousands of saints and martyrs in every generation. We also have our own prayer life, which keeps us in touch with him who is truth and life. "Let us keep our eyes fixed on Jesus, who leads us in our faith and brings it to perfection" (Heb 12:2).

THEORIES AND CRITICS

While biblical criticism came into its own in the twentieth century, it had gone on quietly throughout history. For the sake of brevity here, we shall consider only criticism of the New Testament.

Tatian, around A.D. 175, produced the *Diatesseron*, which is the first attempt at New Testament criticism. It is a harmony of the four Gospels in one continuous text. Origen, who was the head of the famous school of Alexandria, in Egypt, and probably the greatest of the early interpreters of the Bible, used the spiritual meaning of Scripture constantly in his writings. He made extensive use of allegory to illuminate the Old Testament for his Christian audience. He also produced the *Hexapla*, in which he put several Hebrew and Greek texts side by side in six columns in order to compare them.

Eusebius (A.D. 260-340) in his *Church History* gave tables to help see the parallels in the four Gospels. Augustine (A.D. 354-430) saw that the Gospel narratives were the recollections of the church and that the words of Jesus that we read there give his teaching without being a verbatim report.

The Reformers of the sixteenth century insisted on the Bible being translated into the vernacular from the original languages, and that emphasis be given to the literary-historical details. With the dawn of the Enlightenment came the scientific method of studying Scripture. R. Simon, a French priest, was the first to apply the science of historical criticism to the New Testament, which started the ball rolling for today's scholars.

The nineteenth-century critics followed two lines of investigation; one dealt with the historical value of the texts of the New Testament, and the other dealt with the theological value. Before the turn of the twentieth century, some scholars from the German school of Tubingen had already rejected Christ as a real historical person. One of these was B. Baur (1792-1860), who claimed that both Jesus and Paul were literary fictions. From this extreme position things could only improve!

Then came the study of language in the New Testament, helped immensely by the discovery of papyri in Egypt in the late nineteenth century. Since many of these papyri were not biblical texts, they were able to throw light on the times, culture, and languages of the Bible. They showed that the letter form used by Paul, for example, was a normal means of communication for those days.

Scholars also delved into the question of where the evangelists obtained their material. This led to the Two-Source Theory. Remember that a theory is an unproven position, an effort to explain facts with the evidence at hand, so it can never be definitive. The historical-critical method was used to uncover these sources that underlie the Gospel accounts. At this point scholars were on a major quest for the historical Jesus. They succeeded in establishing the priority of Mark and identified a source behind the Gospels as "Q" (from the word Quelle = Source). They determined that both Matthew and Luke used this Q and Mark as sources for their documents. This theory is accepted by many scholars as a "working hypothesis" while more examination goes on. It is by no means accepted by all scholars, but may be taught as "gospel" by some! The sources used for the Gospels probably involve a more complex situation than is presently seen.

THE FORM CRITICS

Next on the scene came form criticism, which seeks to look at the reasons why the early church shaped and transmitted its traditions. It asks what was going on in the Christian community that made this material relevant to them and conditioned the shape in which it was preserved and passed on. These books came out of the church for the church, and therefore reflect its life and conflicts. Paul and the other letter writers, for example, tried to apply the teaching, but also the mind of Christ, to the new situations they found in the early Christian communities. When Paul does not have instructions from the Lord on a certain point, he does not pretend that he has (1 Cor 7:6, 25).

Form criticism examines the period between the Resurrection of Jesus and the first written records, namely A.D. 30 to 80. This covers the foundation of the church, its spread into the Gentile world, and the change from being a Jewish Christian group to a Gentile church. It involved a language change from the Aramaic spoken in Israel to Greek, which was used by most of the new communities. This period also covers the transition from the ministry of Jesus to that of the Apostles, then to their successors, the church's prophets, teachers, and presbyters.

One assumption of the form critics is that the Gospel material would have existed in many small pieces before being assembled into its final form. They distinguish three stages in the development of this material: (1) the context and meaning of a story as it was during the ministry of Jesus; (2) the context of the early church which preserved it and adapted it to the needs of the community; and, (3) the context of the material in the written Gospel. Why, for example, was it put into a particular setting? Does this change its original meaning?

The search for meaning became a full-scale battle when men like R. Bultmann (1884-1976) joined form criticism to theology. The form critics had made some assumptions that paved the way for him. For example, they presumed that oral tradition was important in the early church. So it was, and still is today. Most of what we know about Christianity was passed on to us orally by parents, teachers, and priests.

The form critics presumed that this oral teaching could be detected in the writing of the Gospel, collected, and classified. Furthermore, they thought that these traditions had little or no historical value (here one must be alert) and that the early Christians were not interested in history (in the historian's sense). Thus the Gospels are not biographies of Jesus but reflections of the faith and life of the early church. Since the Christians made no differentiation between Jesus before Calvary and the risen Lord (and why should they?) the form critics say that the early church could freely adapt the material or add to it if they felt so inclined (see *New Jerome Biblical Commentary*, page 1137, art 44).

THE STORM RISES

A word of caution before we proceed. Scientists know that they are limited by the tools they use and by the experiments they carry out. Hammer and chisel will not produce the same results as the scalpel. We can see better with a microscope, but one is limited by the magnification used. Likewise, the literary critics are limited by the tools of their trade and by the presumptions they have going into research.

If you have ever dissected an animal, you are aware of the limitations of instruments—the tools of the scientist. Having exposed all the inner parts that make up the animal, you can point out the circulatory system and all its other physical features. You can write articles on your findings and boast of your knowledge. But you can never retrieve the animal, not even if you sew the whole thing together again. It is sacrificed in the interests of scientific investigation.

When we dissect the Scriptures, we do not have the right to sacrifice God's Word in the interests of scientific investigation. In killing the rabbit there was no fear of killing off the species, but in killing the Word one can do untold damage to people's faith. Both the investigation and the findings of scholars must be shared in an intelligible way with the public. It is destructive for someone to say publicly that Adam and Eve never existed, or that there were no Magi, or worse still that Jesus did not rise from the dead! These statements are simply untrue.

Enter Bultmann, who took the concept of "myth" as the key to interpreting the Gospels. By *myth* he meant the use of imagery to express the other-worldly in this-world terminology. He had no interest in the historical Jesus, and he set about "demythologizing" the Gospels. Heavily influenced by the existentialism of Heidegger, his work created a storm among believers and scholars alike, a storm that guaranteed a good deal of biblical investigation for the rest of the century! He was rejected by fundamentalists and many scholars, although his influence has been immense.

Bultmann claimed that miracles in the Gospels, including the Resurrection, were not reality but myths or imagery used by the evangelists to teach a point. This is the crux of the matter. There were major implications for Christology in eliminating the miraculous, but in doing this he wrote off at least one third of the Gospel as not saying what it clearly was saying.

Since then scholars have taken up different positions regarding the historicity of the texts, yet too many of them are still overly skeptical about the historical value of the tradition. They have gained a reputation for questioning the historicity of the New Testament, and have earned the title "the critics"!

RECENT ADVANCES IN BIBLICAL CRITICISM

With the arrival of the computer and other modern technology biblical research speeded up, with the result that other forms of critical studies developed alongside those mentioned. These include redaction criticism, narrative criticism, canonical criticism, and the use of both sociology and anthropology as interpretive tools to unlock the society that the biblical record speaks about. With these helps scholars try to pry open the ancient world and its secrets for the modern reader.

Redaction criticism has become an important tool of the scholar. According to the dictionary "to redact" means to revise or to edit material. The secretary who takes notes at a meeting and then "writes them up" as the minutes of the next meeting does a work of redaction.

This type of criticism developed from source criticism and form criticism, and came into its own after World War II. Assuming that the sources disclosed by the source critics are reliable, then the redaction critic is interested in the unique views and special emphases that the author imposed on these sources at his disposal. Then he tries to find the life situation in which the biblical writer functioned as well as the theological purpose of his writing.

Both form criticism and redaction criticism begin by trying to distinguish between the traditional material and the editorial material. Source criticism is the necessary preliminary for this process. This is followed by form criticism which concentrates on the pre-literary tradition and ignores the redaction, whereas redaction criticism focusses on the redaction and sets aside the tradition. Form criticism sees the evangelists as mere collectors and collators of tradition, while the redaction critics see the evangelists as real authors. Form criticism deals with the pre-literary stage, while redaction critics deal with the final product.

Redaction criticism has become a popular way of dealing with the text of the New Testament. It allows us to see what the writer did with the existing Christian material available to him. Thus we see the evangelists as interpreters of the tradition, and theologians in their own right.

While redaction criticism has proved its value in practice, there are some problems connected with it. Sometimes these critics go to excess in over-theologizing or psychologizing in trying to tell us the motives and purposes of the authors, and of course there is the problem of reading back into the first century what they did not think of at all.

Narrative criticism deals with "the story" as a technique of writing with its own rules. It too has become a popular way to interpret the text. In this the narrator is seen as omniscient as he alone knows all the facts of the case being related to the reader. He gives psychological insight into the minds of the characters in the scene, speaks to the reader on the side, and arranges the order of the events so that his theological points of view can be communicated.

Canonical critics deal with the biblical book in its context as a part of the canon of Scripture. Their interest is theological rather than literary. The problem is that they can let this issue override the meaning that the book had for the author or his community.

Some anthropological and sociological studies of the 70s while giving insights into the world of the New Testament unfortunately gave rise to terms like "the Jesus movement," or "millenarian sectarians," and even "wandering charismatics" for the early Christians!

When we read books or articles giving us the latest ideas of the scholars, we need to be aware of the fluid nature of these studies. What may be given with certainty today by one, may be contradicted by others as new discoveries are made or as new insights are given. Scholars are aware of the impossibility of being up to date on everything since scholarship had accelerated with the help of technology. They are also aware of their limitations, as scientists are. We need this awareness also as we give mature consideration to their work.

Part IV

The New Testament Is Born

Gospel Beginnings

O VER THE PAST CENTURY serious questions have arisen concerning the authorship and historicity of the Gospels. Some scholars, like Bultmann, have queried whether Jesus ever existed. They have also brought into question the most sacred and cherished doctrines of our faith. So it is important to look into the origins of the Gospels for ourselves. It is no longer enough for us to say that we believe; we must be able to give proofs that our faith is based on fact, not fantasy.

First of all, the "Dogmatic Constitution on Divine Revelation" (Vat II, ch 5:17) asserts that the Church's position with regard to the New Testament remains what it always has been—namely, that it is the record of the fulfillment of God's plan for the redemption of the world. It further states that Jesus is the incarnate Word of God who came to earth to set up God's Kingdom; that he revealed the Father by his words and deeds, and that he accomplished our Redemption by his death on Calvary.

Furthermore, 5:18 states that the church holds to the apostolic origins of the Gospels, which were written under the influence of the Holy Spirit. She affirms that they are historical documents, which means that they are based on real facts, though their authors were free to choose from both oral and written sources suitable to their purpose. Their purpose, which was to reveal the truth to us, was actually achieved. Since the church is the final authority in interpreting the Bible, everything that the scholars say must be read against this yardstick.

DURING JESUS' MINISTRY

There are three important stages in the early church's history. The first is that of the ministry of Jesus, which took place between A.D. 27 and 30. The period from A.D. 30 to 65 covers the ministry of some of the Twelve and of Paul. John, the last Apostle, died in A.D. 98. This was followed by what is now called the Sub-Apostolic Era, between A.D. 65 and 100. The developments in the church in these two latter periods shaped the New Testament.

As far as we know, Jesus did not leave any writings, either in the form of personal letters or teachings. Like the great prophets before him, he committed his teachings to his disciples and trusted them to spread the Word for him. It was a long-standing practice of great teachers to lock up their teachings in the hearts of their disciples (see Is 8:16).

It seems reasonable to suppose that some of the disciples wrote things down during Jesus' ministry, since they knew that they were responsible for passing his teaching on to others. The disciples of the rabbis and of the prophets wrote down the teachings entrusted to them. Some critics claim that the Apostles did not understand Jesus' teaching, nor did they grasp who he was before Calvary, so they could not have written anything. They also claim that the Apostles expected an imminent end to the world, and this would have kept them from writing. Besides, were they not just unlettered fishermen?

The Apostles could certainly have written down incidents and teachings from their contact with Jesus, even if they did not understand them. Even children can do that! Only four of the Apostles were fishermen. Nathanael, "a true Israelite," was most likely an educated one.

Then there was the group of seventy-two (or seventy) disciples who were sent out to preach even during Jesus' own ministry (Lk 10:1-20). To send out thirty-six pairs of disciples to all the villages and towns of Israel would have required quite a bit of preparation and instruction. They must have been given a "package" of teaching to present to the people. They would have to explain who Jesus was and why he came and give examples of his teaching. A few phrases regarding the coming of the Messiah would not get them very far.

Moreover, Jesus ordered these disciples as well as the Twelve to heal, exorcise spirits, and raise the dead (Lk 10:1-20; Mt 10:8; Mk 6:7-13). To have the impact on Israel that the Gospels claim—namely, that the nation was in a ferment regarding Jesus—these disciples would have had to meet regularly to gather their material together and to have it explained. It would be amazing if none of them wrote anything down. We remember only about one-third of any teaching given orally. If the teaching of Jesus was not to be lost, someone must have written it down even at this early stage.

A NEW UNDERSTANDING FROM THE MASTER

In Israel at that time, as in many parts of the world today, everything closed at sundown. There would be plenty of time for the disciples of Jesus to gather in the long evenings to discuss, to question Jesus on the implications of his teaching, and to establish its connection with the Old Testament prophecies regarding the Coming One (see Mt 13:36-37). Many of these early disciples would have known Jesus' mother, Mary, and from her would have gleaned the knowledge of his early days and youth in Nazareth. Human nature demands such information regarding its heroes, even in our sophisticated technical age. Jesus must have guided their thinking on this, for he certainly did so after the Resurrection (see Lk 24:27, 44).

Even though Jesus prepared his disciples for his passion and death, it is clear from the Gospels that they they could not grasp what he was saying. Israel was expecting a Messiah who would save them politically. Part of the nation's anger against Jesus was the fact that he refused to satisfy them on this count. The events of Good Friday both shattered and scattered the disciples, but Jesus' Resurrection transformed their understanding. *In this light* all his teaching made sense. They saw his death now as that of the Paschal Lamb who had given his life for the Redemption of everyone, and the Resurrection proved his claim to divinity.

Luke 24:25 says that Jesus himself gave the Apostles a new understanding of Scripture when he personally taught them during the forty days after the Resurrection. He guided them in a Christological interpretation of the Old Testament: "Then he said to them, 'You foolish men! So slow to believe all that the prophets have said! Was it not necessary that the Christ should suffer before entering into his glory?' Then, starting with Moses and going through all the prophets, he explained to them the passages throughout the scriptures that were about himself."

THE CHURCH BEGINS

After Pentecost, the next major breakthrough, the Apostles went out to preach Christ to Israel. Almost everyone in Israel knew, to their cost, who Jesus of Nazareth was. The nation had been through a crisis over him. All Jerusalem (a very small city even by ancient standards) had witnessed his ministry there and his deliberate entry into the city as its King-Messiah. They had both witnessed and participated in his death. There was no need, therefore, for Peter or the other Apostles to tell them the details of Jesus' life, but it was necessary to interpret him. Israel had not understood Jesus at all, nor accepted his claims.

Some examples of this early preaching are given in Acts chapters 2 through 8, where the Apostles cite the Old Testament Scriptures to explain Christ to Israel. The Resurrection is the key to that understanding, the one fact that throws light on all other facts and also proves Jesus' claim to divinity. The Apostles offer themselves as witnesses to the Resurrection, not because they saw what happened in the tomb on Easter morning, but because they had seen and heard the risen Lord for themselves. At this point they are the primary witnesses to both his ministry and his Resurrection (Acts 2:32).

If the Resurrection had not happened, then the extraordinary transformation of these disciples, who hid "for fear of the Jews" (Jn 20:19) after the death of Jesus, would be inexplicable.

It was the Resurrection and its aftermath, the coming of the Holy Spirit upon the church, that changed the Apostles and other disciples into bold witnesses. They went out to preach that Jesus really was the Messiah sent by God and that it was not too late to believe in him. God had not intended to send a military or political leader, for that would only have temporary effects. Instead he sent a spiritual Messiah who liberated us from the real slavery to sin.

Jesus' forgiveness of sinners was public knowledge (Lk 7:34). Now Israel hears that because he is God, alive, and their victorious Lamb (Rv 5), forgiveness is universally available to all sinners, even to those responsible for his death. The house of mercy was to be found in the loving heart of Jesus, the Savior.

The Apostles did not give a list of the miracles of Jesus, for their own ministry *was a continuation of his* (see Acts 3, 8, 9, 14).

They did not list his teachings, for they continued to teach them. They understood that he was the head of the body to which they belonged by virtue of their baptism. There was, therefore, no break between the ministry of Jesus and that of the Apostles. He was the vine of which they were the branches, so their ministry *was* his (see Jn 14:12; Mk 16:20).

THE GOSPEL TO THE NATIONS

Initially most Christians lived in or around Jerusalem. Acts 2 testifies to the fact that on Pentecost day there were people listening to Peter from all of the known world at that time. They came from the south: from North Africa, Egypt, Cyrene, and Libya. Others came from the north: from the regions of Asia, Phrygia, Pamphylia, Cappadocia, and Pontus, which the church was to visit soon on its missionary journeys. They came also from Mesopotamia in the east, the Elamites, the Medes, and the Parthians. Crete and Rome represented the west side. Acts 2:41 says that a vast number, about three thousand people, were converted that day. Thus we are given a picture of a church ready to burst upon the world when these people returned to their homelands. They prepared the ground for later visits by the Apostles.

The church in Jerusalem was the mother church for a long time, with the Apostle James as its leader. Initially everything was coordinated from there, for Peter and John resided there also. Eventually persecution drove the Christians out of Jerusalem (Acts 6-7) into other regions, resulting in other centers becoming important, especially Antioch in Syria.

It is obvious from this, and from what was said previously, that most of the preaching could not be done by twelve men, no matter how great they were. It became necessary for them to do what the Master had done for them. They had to train others and appoint them to various church responsibilities (see Acts 6:1-6). The gospel would henceforth be preached by a host of evangelists, prophets, preachers, and teachers who were not the primary witnesses to Jesus (see Eph 4:11-12). These people needed written accounts of the life and teaching of Jesus to pass on to others. Oral teaching would not be enough. They would need documents authenticated by the Apostles in order to silence objectors and prevent false teaching from developing.

RELIABLE WITNESSES

They would have had two primary sources of information, namely Mary, the mother of Jesus, and Jesus' disciples. Tradition says that Mary lived to be sixty-four years old. She would have been approximately forty-eight years of age when Jesus died. She had some time to help get the church on its feet. She would be the prime source of information on the infancy and youth of Jesus, and she would have had recollections of the ministry, passion, death, and Resurrection also. Since these observations cannot be verified by textual evidence or by archeology, the literary critics will not consider them. For them, the last appearance of Mary in the texts is on Pentecost day (Acts 2), so this is all they have to work with.

The other source of information was the Twelve and the seventy-two who were involved in the ministry of Jesus. Then, of course, many people who had been healed by Jesus were alive and could give their own witness, like the family of Lazarus. In A.D. 57 Paul claimed that most of those who had seen the risen Lord were still alive (1 Cor 15:6).

It must have become important for the scribes in the church to write down all that these witnesses remembered. In those days people's power of recall was much greater than ours, for they had no mechanical means of retaining information. It was perfectly normal, for example, for a Jewish boy of twelve to be able to recite the Pentateuch by heart! In this context we can be sure that they remembered quite accurately what Jesus had said and done. From this arose a body of material (not in book form yet), which became the treasure of the church and the source material from which the evangelists drew when writing their individual Gospels. Luke 1:1 testifies that many had undertaken to write about the events pertaining to Christ. Some of this material may still await discovery.

It was not enough to tell the stories accurately. They had to be interpreted and explained "according to the Scriptures" (see 1 Cor 15:3-4). At this stage also the new communities of Asia Minor, as well as those from all the other places not specifically mentioned, needed to have both written and oral teaching to nourish their churches. Copies would have been made, and the local teachers and preachers would interpret the texts, as happens everywhere even today.

I will deal with the actual writing of the Gospels in chapters 14 and 15. Now I want to turn to the Epistles, the first writings of the New Testament.

FOURTEEN

The New Testament Letters

O NE OF THE MOST DECISIVE MOMENTS in the early church was the conversion of Paul around A.D. 34. His meeting with the risen Lord on the Damascus road opened his mind to the truth of the Christian faith. Born in Tarsus of Cilicia, he understood the need to take the gospel to the far-flung regions of the Roman Empire, of which he was a citizen. He was called to be the missionary to the Gentiles (Acts 9; Gal 1).

After several years in Arabia meditating on the new realities opened up to him, Paul went back to Damascus to preach. In approximately A.D. 39 he made a brief visit to Jerusalem. The Christians were afraid of him at this time because of his previous persecution of the church (Acts 9:26-31). So Paul returned to Tarsus, where he spent the next seven years. But God turns everything out for the good for those who love him (Rom 8:28-29). Paul's long stay at Tarsus gave him time to pray and meditate on the Old Testament Scriptures. The depths of thought that later appeared in his writings are due to these silent years.

THE FIRST MISSIONARIES

Paul remained in Tarsus until Antioch needed a dynamic leader, one who had vision, courage, and energy. Barnabas was sent by the Apostles in Jerusalem to discern what was going on there (Acts 11:22-26), and he decided the situation needed Paul. There were other centers of the church in Samaria (Acts 8) and Damascus (Acts 9), but Antioch took precedence over them as a major center for the conversion of the Gentiles. There, around A.D. 36, the followers of Jesus first became known as "Christians," meaning "followers of the Christ" (Messiah). This would never have happened in a Jewish context.

The Christian missionaries passed on to their converts the Old Testament, as well as the teaching of Jesus. The Old Testament was understood to be the foundation for the mystery of Christ. They used the Septuagint, the Greek translation, as it was the most available and it was in the language of the people.

The Old Testament would have been familiar to the Gentiles in Asia Minor because there were Jewish colonies everywhere. As the Apostles admitted in their very first official letter to the churches, "Moses has always had his preachers in every town and is read aloud in the synagogues every Sabbath" (Acts 15:21). Many Gentiles believed in the true God but did not want to become members of the Jewish race. They refused circumcision and were known as God Fearers. Another group called the "Freedmen" had purchased their freedom from their masters. Both of these groups attended the synagogues and were well-versed in the Old Testament. They welcomed the Christian missionaries, and many of them became Christians.

Paul and Barnabas formed a missionary team and began preaching in Cyprus, Asia Minor (modern Turkey), Macedonia, and Achaia (modern Greece). They eventually formed two teams and others joined them. Everywhere they went they founded churches and appointed pastors and teachers to guide them. Paul was quite clear that he had a tradition to pass on to his new churches, for he spoke of a body of material that was passed on to him after his conversion and which he in turn now passed on to them, to be guarded and treasured and held for posterity. For example, in writing to the Corinthians (1 Cor 11:2), he congratulated them for "maintaining the traditions exactly as I passed them on to you." Likewise in 1 Corinthians 15:3-7, he repeats verbatim what he had been taught himself, namely, that Christ died for our sins "in accordance with the Scriptures." In verse 3 he refers to "the tradition I handed on to you in the first place, a tradition I had myself first received."

It is interesting to note that Paul, converted so soon after the Resurrection, speaks about a fixed tradition that nobody can change. He can explain it but not alter it. When writing to the Thessalonians (2 Thes 2:15), he says that they are to "keep the traditions that we taught you, whether by word of mouth or by letter," for as he says in 1 Thessalonians 4:1-2, "you are well aware of the instructions we gave you on the authority of the Lord Jesus." In 2 Corinthians 11:4 Paul speaks of a specific "gospel" which cannot be changed. Clearly, then, the Christian missionaries taught not only by word of mouth, but also passed on whatever was written down by the earliest witnesses. Not only the memoirs but also the way of life taught by Jesus were considered unalterable (2 Thes 3:6).

EARLIEST CHRISTIAN WRITINGS THAT SURVIVED

Not everything that was written has survived the passage of time. The first letter ever written to the churches has survived because Luke enshrined it in Acts 15:22-29. It was written after the Council of Jerusalem (A.D. 48), when Paul and Barnabas met with the Apostles in Jerusalem to discuss the question of Gentiles in the church. It was at this meeting that Paul and Barnabas were accepted as the Apostles to the Gentiles (Gal 2), on an equal footing with the other Apostles of the Lord. They were given a letter to take to the churches to make table fellowship between Jews and Gentiles easier. It did not demand circumcision for Gentiles, thus releasing the church from becoming a sect of Judaism.

There are several groups of letters found in the New Testament: (1) the Pauline Corpus, (2) the Pastorals, (3) the Johannine Corpus, (4) the Catholic Epistles, (5) the Letter to the Hebrews.

PAUL'S LETTERS

These consist of 1 and 2 Thessalonians, 1 and 2 Corinthians, Galatians, Romans, Philippians, Colossians, Ephesians, and Philemon. These letters are Paul's responses to questions or problems from the various churches.

Paul's first letters were written to Thessalonica, in northern Macedonia, around A.D. 50. He wanted to encourage his converts to remain faithful under persecution. He also calmed their fears with regard to the Second Coming, which some of them thought was imminent. Paul had no sympathy for those who had given up their normal occupations to sit around waiting for Jesus to return. He knew from Jesus' teaching that his return would be sudden, and that he expected to find his servants doing God's will (Mt 24:47).

The Letters to the Corinthians were written in A.D. 57. Corinth, a cosmopolitan city that attracted every sort of religion and philosophy, was notorious for its immorality. Paul founded a fervent Christian community that was very charismatic in style. But these Corinthians certainly proved Paul's gifts as a pastor and theologian, for no church tested him as much as they did, and on so many issues. We can be grateful to them, for otherwise we would not have the great wisdom found in these letters, which deal with such diverse subjects as marriage and virginity (1 Cor 7), moral conduct (1 Cor 5-6), the Eucharist, (1 Cor 11), charismatic gifts (1 Cor 12-14), and the Resurrection (1 Cor 15).

Paul demanded that for Corinth, as for Christ himself, love should reign supreme in every aspect of life (1 Cor 13). This teaching was sent to a city known for its corruption! It's as if Paul was saying, "You want love? Well, I will explain what real love is, and then I dare you to live it!" In 2 Corinthians Paul deals with the Christian way of handling suffering and the glory of being an apostle for Christ. He also uses a money collection to teach about generosity. Paul's genius was able to turn what could have been a dry case of conscience into a vehicle of profound revelation about Christ and the Christian way of life.

Galatians was written around A.D. 54 and Romans around A.D. 58. Both letters deal with the same problems, though Galatians was written in answer to a real need and Romans represents Paul's distilled thought on the matter, written to a church he had never visited but hoped to visit soon. In these letters Paul contrasts the goodness that people can achieve by their own efforts with the holiness that comes through Christ. It is the contrast between the immorality of the pagan world and the glory of the life in Christ described in Romans 8. The place of the law is clearly shown, in contrast with the glory of faith in Christ. These letters are "vintage Paul."

Philippians was written in A.D. 56 or 57. Here Paul speaks of being under arrest. This is often assumed to be the Roman house arrest of Acts 28, but the ease with which he can contact the church at Philippi would seem strange at that distance. This letter was more likely written at the time of his earlier detention in Caesarea (Acts 24:22-27). He wrote a friendly letter to encourage the Philippians' faith under difficult circumstances. There are some celebrated passages in this letter, such as the hymn to Christ in chapter 2 and Paul's own statement of commitment in chapter 3.

Ephesians and Colossians are dated between A.D. 61 and 63, the time of the Roman arrest. Philemon could be placed with either of the detention dates, 56 to 57 or 61 to 63.

These letters are related, for the mission that Onesimus is sent on in Colossians 4:9 is the same as in Philemon 10 to 12.

The Letter to Philemon is the only personal letter of Paul to an individual that is extant. Here we see him plead for a poor runaway slave to be accepted back as a Christian brother by his former master. The Letters to the Colossians and Ephesians have the same relationship as that of Galatians and Romans. What is written to the church of Colossae, one that Paul did not found, is further developed in Ephesians, which is really a letter to the whole church. Some modern critics have called Paul's authorship of Ephesians into question, but this letter has always been ascribed by the church to Paul.

In these letters Paul sets forth the supremacy of Christ over every power in the universe. Christ is the Lord of the cosmos, the fullness of God, and the church is his body. Paul's thought soars to new heights here. He was obviously responding to people who acknowledged powers in the universe other than Christ. These challenges to Christ's lordship made Paul consider Christ on a cosmic level, something he did not have to do before. His discussions of the supremacy of Christ in the first chapters of Colossians and Ephesians are truly magnificent.

THE PASTORALS

The Letters to Timothy and Titus are dated by some critics between A.D. 65 and 80; by others as late as A.D. 100. They are said to be written by disciples of Paul, who used his name in order to have more authority in the communities involved. Tradition held that these letters were Pauline because the author claims to be Paul, but the church situation in these letters appears to be much more structured and perhaps more settled than in Paul's day.

A more conservative dating places 1 Timothy and Titus in

A.D. 65 and 2 Timothy in A.D. 66 or 67, thus owning Pauline authorship. In 2 Timothy 4:16 Paul speaks about a recent hearing of his case. A disciple would hardly need to refer to this after Paul's death. (This is an example of the confusion of opinion one meets within New Testament studies today.) An important point to remember is that if all of the letters mentioned so far were written before A.D. 63, then an extraordinary amount of development—both in theology and in church structure—had taken place quite rapidly. This has a bearing on the development of the Gospels, as we shall see.

THE CATHOLIC LETTERS

As we move into this section it is well to remember two major events that affected the church at this time. One was the dreadful persecution under Nero and his subsequent suicide in A.D. 68. The other was the fall of Jerusalem in A.D. 70. The great fire of Rome, said to have been started by the emperor himself, occurred in 64. The emperor in turn blamed the Christians for the fire, thus deflecting attention from himself and turning the anger of Rome against the church. During this persecution both Peter and Paul were martyred, Peter in A.D. 65 and Paul in 67. It is against this background that we must look at the Petrine Letters.

The Letters of Peter, James, and Jude are called "catholic" or universal as they are not specifically addressed to any one community or situation. Two letters bear Peter's name. Most scholars accept Peter as the author of the first, but authorship of the second one was questioned from the early days of the church. Most scholars believe that it was written by a disciple using Peter's teaching, and also using the letter of Jude and other texts as his sources.

First Peter is dated A.D. 64 (although critics who reject Petrine authorship date it A.D. 70 to 80). It encourages

Christians who are suffering for their faith to persevere, for their calling is a great one (1 Pt 4:12). Peter soon afterwards gave them the example of one who persevered unto death in fidelity to the Master.

Second Peter is dated later, and consists of warnings against false teachers. It also tries to quiet anxieties regarding the delayed Second Coming of Jesus. This letter quotes that of Jude and speaks of an accepted Pauline Corpus in the church.

The Letter of James claims to have apostolic authorship also. This James was the "brother of the Lord" (Gal 1:19; Mk 6:3) and leader of the church in Jerusalem (Acts 12:17; 15:13). He is writing authoritatively to the twelve tribes of the Dispersion, therefore to the Jewish Christians (1:1). Since James the brother of John, the son of Zebedee, was martyred in Jerusalem in A.D. 44 by Herod Agrippa I (Acts 12:2), this James must be the son of Alphaeus (Acts 1:13), who was a cousin of Jesus. He was known to the later church as "James the Just" (Eusebius: *Church History* 2.23).

This letter must have been written before 62, the date of James's martyrdom at the hand of the Jews. Its teaching reflects the earlier rather than later struggles in the church. It appears to reflect a stage when there was as yet no break between church and synagogue. Some even suggest that it might reflect the struggles before the Council of Jerusalem (in 48), which would make it the oldest Christian writing.

In this letter James challenges Paul on the question of faith versus good works. (Perhaps he was not so much challenging Paul himself as those who distorted his teaching?) A faith that does nothing to show its love for God or neighbor is unacceptable for Christians. We have the example of Jesus, who "went about doing good" (Acts 10:38).

The Letter of Jude also claims apostolic authorship. He is the brother of the Lord and also, perhaps, brother of James (Mt 13:55). This letter denounces false teachers and warns them of divine punishment if they lead the flock of God astray. It is usually dated fairly late (70 to 90), which would mean that the letter as we have it now is later than the Apostle who bears its name.

THE LETTER TO THE HEBREWS

Traditionally this has been classed with the Pauline Corpus, but the Fathers of the church accepted it as canonical without knowing who wrote it. The suggested author is Apollos, the Alexandrian Jew whose fluency and eloquence in Scripture was both recognized and praised in the early church (Acts 18:24-28). Critics differ as to the dating of the letter: A.D. 67 is a reasonable date, since the author speaks of the Jerusalem temple as still in operation but soon to disappear (8:13). This would be a pointless statement if the event were past. In Hebrews 9:8 he says that the "old tent," meaning Judaism, still stands. These Hebrews have suffered since they became Christians (10:32), but must not give up now (13:7-8). This letter is perhaps addressed to Jewish Christians in Rome who have survived the Neronian persecution so far. Nero has not yet died, however, thus giving 67 as a plausible date of writing.

The Hebrews' theme is that of the eternal priesthood of Christ, and the argument is based completely on the Old Testament. It presumes a thorough knowledge and understanding of the old covenant and the Jewish system of worship. It was therefore obviously addressed to Jewish Christians, to encourage them to understand the preeminence of Christ's priesthood and sacrifice over those of the Mosaic covenant. They had lost nothing but gained everything in going over to Christ, the fulfillment of all that their people held dear.

FIFTEEN

Three Gospels and Acts

T HE THREE GOSPELS OF Matthew, Mark, and Luke are said to
be synoptic because they have so much material in
common. Scholars believe that Mark was the first to be
completed. Tradition in the early church is unanimous in
attributing the Gospel to Mark—that is, the John Mark of
Acts 12:12, 25; 13:5-13; 15:37-39; and Colossians 4:10.

THE GOSPEL OF MARK

The earliest witness is Papias, bishop of Phrygia in Asia
Minor in A.D. 120. Papias is quoted by Eusebius (*Church
History* 3.39) as saying that Mark became Peter's interpreter.
He wrote down all that he remembered of what the Lord
had said and done, but he did not write the events in
chronological order. Peter adapted his teaching to the needs
of his audience, so Mark, in recording these teachings of
Peter, was not distorting the message of the Lord. The *Anti-
Marcionite Prologue* (A.D. 160-180) says that Mark was called
"stump-fingered" because his fingers were short in relation
to the rest of his body. After Peter's death he wrote down
this Gospel in the region of Italy. Jerome agrees with the
above, but adds that the church at Rome requested Mark to

write the Gospel and that Peter approved.

Mark's Gospel was written for Gentile Christians, so he explains Jewish customs in the text (7:3; 14:12; 15:42), as well as expressions like "Boanerges," which means "sons of thunder" (3:17; see also 5:41; 7:11, 34; 14:36; 15:22, 34). There is almost unanimous agreement that the Gospel was written before A.D. 70, during the Jewish war that issued in the destruction of Jerusalem. Since tradition situates Peter's martyrdom in 64, the Gospel was probably finalized between A.D. 65 and 70.

The source material available to Mark would have been both written and oral tradition. The Aramaic Gospel of Matthew, which I will explain further in the section on the Gospel of Matthew, was already in circulation. Mark also had the teaching of Peter and whatever collections of writings were currently in use. It seems from the Gospels that there was a passion narrative in circulation from a very early stage, and that the church leaders never ceased to meditate on its significance. Hence the passion narratives have a coherence that is lacking in the Resurrection accounts, for example. Many of the incidents related in Mark have the vivid details of an eyewitness account. He could only have gotten these from Peter himself, who relived the various scenes as he described them to his audiences.

It is a well-known fact that the Gospels are not just narratives of what happened "back there" in the life and ministry of Jesus. The evangelists had no interest in giving us a biography of Jesus, just the kerygma. The Apostles were very anxious for Christians to continue the work of Jesus, so they interpreted him for them, on the understanding that the branches should be like the vine. Therefore the Gospels are complex theological works that reveal the significance of the life and work of Jesus and of his body, the church. The material is adapted to this purpose. We must read them thus in order to understand them, for this is understanding the mind of the authors.

Mark's presentation of Jesus is that of the lowly servant of

God, the one who came to do the whole will of God and who proved who he was by his works alone. We are given a one-sentence introduction to him as the Son of God and then catapulted into the ministry. The Servant Songs of Isaiah appear to influence Mark's presentation of Jesus, the servant who would redeem us by suffering after he had served in a wonderful miracle ministry.

In Isaiah 42:1-9 the servant is the Lord's delight, the one on whom the Spirit rests (see Mk 1:11; 9:8). He brings true justice to the nations and works miracles. Isaiah 49:1-6 says that although the servant will suffer, he is nevertheless the true light of the nations. Isaiah 50:4-11 has the suffering described more explicitly, and also includes an exhortation to follow the servant. Isaiah 52:13-53:12 gives the full suffering and triumph of the servant of the Lord.

Since the presentation of Jesus is that of the suffering servant of God, there is no genealogy given, for no one is interested in the genealogy of servants. We are interested only in their work, so thirteen of the sixteen chapters of Mark relate the work of Jesus. He even works from Heaven with the church in Mark 16:20.

Chapter one gives what could reasonably be called "a day in the life of Jesus of Nazareth," and it emphasizes the long hours of work for the sake of others. The obedient servant carries out his mission for the Father against all odds and at any price. God's servant is not understood, either in himself or in his mission. He cannot allow them to call him "Messiah," for their understanding of that word is both political and military. Hence the so-called "messianic secret" of Mark's Gospel, where Jesus is revealed as the Messiah only at the time of his passion.

It is significant that Mark emphasizes the suffering of Jesus and his abandonment by everyone, including the sense of the loss of God's presence while dying on the cross, but he gives only a brief announcement of the Resurrection. His Gospel ends abruptly with the women running away from the tomb on Easter day. At a later stage the church added 16:9-20 as a summary of the Resurrection appearances. These verses testify to the fact that the church remembered the Resurrection appearances in a certain sequence.

It appears that Mark was writing for a church that was suffering deeply. The dating implies the Neronian persecution. Peter had just been martyred, and Paul was to follow in A.D. 67. The strong emphasis on the suffering of Jesus and on his servant role makes more sense in this light. Mark insists on discipleship throughout his Gospel. In the beginning the disciples leave all to follow Jesus (1:16-20), but as the passion approaches they leave all to desert him! The emphasis on Peter's denials and Judas's betrayal make sense here, for there were lessons to learn from both.

The lack of emphasis on the Resurrection accounts is due to the fact that, for Mark, the risen Jesus is among them, and they don't need visions to prove it. He had told them that he was going before them into Galilee, and they would meet him there (16:7-8). For Mark, "Galilee" is a symbol of the mission of the church.

Only a few privileged witnesses saw Jesus after the Resurrection. That gift was not given to all, for we are to walk by faith and not by sight. It is the indwelling presence of Jesus in the church that is all important. This presence ensures that those undergoing persecution are not without the help of the Lord in their necessities. There is no need for further denials and betrayals among Christians; the lessons of the past have been learned. They have the example of Peter, who has died for the one whom he earlier denied.

THE GOSPEL OF MATTHEW

Early church tradition is unanimous in claiming that Matthew, the tax collector and Apostle of Jesus, wrote a Gospel in Aramaic for the Hebrew Christians. He may not have written a full Gospel (as we know them today), for Papias (Eusebius, *Church History* 3.39) says that "Matthew wrote the oracles [sayings of Jesus] in the Hebrew language, and everyone interpreted them as he was able." Irenaeus in the second century says that Matthew wrote while Peter and Paul worked in the church at Rome, therefore prior to A.D. 64. Eusebius and Origen in the third century say the same. Today it is assumed to have been written between A.D. 30 and 50.

The problem is that this Aramaic text is lost. Perhaps this was the source that the synoptic Gospels all used, the so-called "Q" text? As Papias said, it would have had to be translated into the Greek language almost immediately so that it could be used in the churches. Jerome, when commenting on the Aramaic Gospel of Matthew in the fourth century, said that whenever Matthew quoted the Old Testament, he used the Hebrew text, not the Septuagint. This is an important point for scholars, especially for the interpretation of Isaiah 7:14 in 1:23.

The Gospel that we have under the same name was written in Greek by an obviously learned scribe, steeped in the Old Testament Scriptures. He used the Gospel of Mark, some traditions that Luke also used, in addition to Matthew's Aramaic Gospel. The end product is a new Gospel by this unknown author, under Matthew's name. The date of composition of Greek Matthew would have been somewhere between A.D. 70 and 80. The concern is still for Jewish Christians, who are now expelled from Palestine and must find their home among Gentile Christians.

The presentation of Jesus in Matthew is that of the King-Messiah foretold by the prophets. To make his point Matthew quotes the Old Testament more than forty times, citing prophecy and its fulfillment. Since Jesus is the prince of the house of David, a royal genealogy is given. The teaching and parables reveal what the Kingdom of Heaven is like, and the Sermon on the Mount reveals the new law of that Kingdom. Like Moses, Jesus is the uncrowned ruler of Israel. Moreover, he is the rejected King, crowned only in mockery and enthroned only on a cross of shame. But in the end he is the glorious, victorious King who sends out his messengers to conquer the world in his name.

Matthew's Gospel shows a keen interest in the church. It reveals a church that has developed its structures and is quite organized in its life. Many consider this Gospel a handbook for church leaders.

Matthew organized his material into five sections, in imitation of the Pentateuch. He has five discourses, each with its own narrative section: the evangelistic discourse, with its narrative promulgating the Kingdom of Heaven (Mt 3-7); the apostolic discourse, including ten miracles (Mt 8-10); the parabolic discourse, with its narrative on the mystery of the Kingdom of Heaven (Mt 11:1-13:52); the ecclesiastical discourse, pertaining to church matters (Mt 13:53-18); and finally the eschatalogical discourse, with its passion and Resurrection narratives (Mt 19-28).

THE GOSPEL OF LUKE

Early tradition is unanimous in attributing this Gospel to Luke, who was a companion of Paul. Irenaeus (second century) and the *Anti-Marcionite Prologue* (A.D. 160-180) both testify to Luke's authorship. Other ancient testimonies to Lukan authorship are the Muratorian Canon (second century) and Jerome (fourth century).

The *Anti-Marcionite Prologue* states that Luke was a Syrian from Antioch, a doctor by profession, and a disciple of the Apostles. Later he was a companion of Paul (see Col 4:14; Phlm 23; 2 Tm 4:11). He was celibate all his life, and died full of the Spirit in Boeotia at the age of eighty-four. It further states that Luke wrote after Matthew's Gospel had been written in Judea, and Mark's in Italy. Luke wrote in the region of

Achaia (southern Greece). He was anxious to render the gospel message to Gentiles, as Matthew had done for the Jews. Later he also wrote the Acts of the Apostles.

Luke-Acts is presented as a two-volume work dedicated to a certain Theophilus, which means "lover of God." Luke could have written "Dear Christian" instead, for his works have a universalist vision that is truly refreshing. Writing for Gentile Christians, Luke presents Jesus as God's ideal man, everything God wanted in a Son and servant. His Gospel could be entitled "Behold the Man!" or even "What a Man!" He portrays Jesus as the man of prayer, the man of compassion, the man of courage, the man who loved the poor, who healed the sick, who raised the dead, who forgave, restored, and transformed sinners.

Since the humanity of Jesus is stressed, the genealogy presented is a human one that traces Jesus back to Adam and then to God, for the man "Christ Jesus was like unto us in all things except sin only" (Heb 2:17; 4:15). Jesus is also the shepherd who collects into his fold all those whom nobody else wants, such as the tax collectors, the prostitutes, and the "good" thief. This wonderfully comforting Gospel pictures God as the loving one who is near us, to listen to us and heal our ills.

Yet this Gospel is not all comfort. It contains a radical demand for disciples to follow the Master in his life of poverty, selflessness, and giving to others. No one reading Luke's demands to give away all material possessions can be comfortable! The proper use of money is to give it away, for we follow the Master who even gave up his life for us. The Gospel of Luke is unique in its infancy narrative. We will deal with this in chapter 17.

THE ACTS OF THE APOSTLES

Luke's work was completed between A.D. 70 and 90, after the destruction of Jerusalem and the dispersion of the Jews.

The oldest view of the church is that Luke wrote Acts in Achaia sometime after Paul's death in A.D. 67. It must therefore have the same dating as his Gospel. Until recently no one questioned Luke's authorship. Some scholars today claim that the writer is unknown, coming from a church where Paul had been the Apostle.

As the Acts clearly claims to be a continuation of the Gospel, it can only be understood as such. The Gospel tells the story of the Christ from his birth to the Ascension. Acts takes up from that point to show that the church did, in fact, spread into the whole world. The same universalist vision is found in Acts as in the Gospel, for both are interested in presenting salvation history. The author is not interested in personalities as such, but in showing the church spreading out into all the world.

Many consider it curious that Luke did not give details of the deaths of either Peter or Paul, the two great Apostles of Acts. Luke could have finished his book just after Paul's arrival in Rome in A.D. 61. This would explain why there are no reports of the deaths of Peter and Paul or the destruction of Jerusalem, all of which were major events that affected Christians. On the other hand, Luke is interested in the spread of the gospel, not in biographies. Peter and Paul are servants of the Lord; their deaths do not constitute the death of the church. It must continue to preach the gospel to every nation and generation.

Once the church reaches the center of the Roman Empire, Luke stops abruptly. At that time Rome was the hub of the known world, and Luke may have assumed we would know that whatever Rome espoused would be taken to the ends of the earth. Luke seems to say also that the Second Coming is not imminent, that the church must settle in "for the long haul." The missionary activity of Peter and Paul must be picked up by others now, and taken to the farthest reaches of the globe.

SIXTEEN

Writings of John, the Beloved

I T HAS LONG BEEN RECOGNIZED that the Johannine tradition is unique and also separate from the tradition found in the other Gospels. It is generally accepted that the Apostle John, the beloved disciple of Jesus, lies behind this tradition. The works include the Gospel of John, the Letters of John, and the Book of Revelation, also called the Apocalypse.

THE GOSPEL OF JOHN

Evidence of John as Author. Although modern scholars doubt John's authorship of this Gospel, the weight of tradition favors him as the àuthor. The *Anti-Marcionite Prologues* state that "the Apostle John wrote his Apocalypse on the Island of Patmos, and then his gospel in Asia. The gospel of John was published and given to the churches by John while still in the body, as Papias of Hierapolis, a dear disciple of John, recorded." The Muratorian Canon (A.D. 180-200) says that "the fourth gospel is that of John, one of the disciples." Irenaeus (A.D. 180) in his work "Against Heresies" (3:1) states, "Afterwards, John the disciple of the Lord, who had leaned upon his breast, did himself publish a gospel during his residence at Ephesus in Asia." Clement of Alexandria in A.D. 211 said that "last of all, John, perceiving that the external facts had been made plain in the gospel, being urged by his friends, and inspired by the Spirit, composed a spiritual gospel."

Lastly, Jerome in A.D. 398 said in his commentary on the Gospel of Matthew: "The last is John, the apostle and evangelist, whom Jesus loved most, who, reclining on the Lord's bosom, drank the purest streams of doctrine, and was the only one thought worthy of the words from the cross, 'Behold! Your mother.' When he was in Asia, at the time when the seeds of heresy were springing up (I refer to Cerinthus, Ebion, and the rest who say that Christ has not come in the flesh, whom he in his own epistle calls Antichrists, and whom the apostle Paul frequently assails), he was urged by almost all the bishops in Asia then living, and by deputations from many churches, to write more profoundly concerning the divinity of the Savior, and to break through all obstacles so as to attain to the very Word of God."

Jerome also says that John wrote the Apocalypse from the Island of Patmos during the persecution of Domition. After Domition had been put to death, John returned to Asia, where he continued to found and build churches throughout all Asia until he died of old age in the sixty-eighth year after the Lord's passion (A.D. 98). He was then buried in Ephesus. John's Gospel was therefore written by the Apostle in Ephesus and completed about A.D. 95.

Modern Scholars Debate. This conclusion is not the same as that of modern scholarship, however, which operates from the various forms of literary and biblical criticism. These scholars claim that the author is anonymous, coming from the "Johannine School," and that the work represents a whole church rather than an individual (Jn 21:24). They acknowledge that the final draft is definitely the work of an individual, obviously a spiritual genius and a theological giant.

This scholarly theory is unnecessary when John fits the description fully. Those inclined to date John very late have been challenged by a recent discovery in Egypt of a fragment copied from the original and dating from A.D. 130. Allowing time for the Gospel to have been copied and distributed throughout the church, the earlier dating is better.

An Eyewitness Account. We can see signs of John's hand in this work. He, like Peter, was an Apostle to the Jews (Gal 2:9), until he went to Ephesus later in life. He worked in both Jerusalem and Samaria in the early years (Acts 3-4; 8:14-25). Like Acts 1:8, this Gospel follows the spread of the church from Jerusalem (Jn 2-3) to Samaria (Jn 4)—from the mission to the Jews to that of the half-Jews and then the Gentiles, represented by the man in John 4:43-54. The author speaks as an eyewitness. For instance, in John 5:2 he speaks of a sheep pool in Jerusalem as if it is still in existence. This place was destroyed with the fall of Jerusalem in 70, and only uncovered in the twentieth century by archeologists.

John 6:15 witnesses to an event not referred to in the synoptics. It says that after the miracle of the loaves, the people were not just excited by a miraculous event; they wanted to declare Jesus King of the Jews! The situation was suddenly transformed into a very dangerous political moment, and Jesus, who knew that he could not reason with the crowd, had to escape into the hills for safety.

This is not just "a stray piece of tradition" but the report of someone who was there and who appreciated the danger for Jesus. In the passion narrative John is most careful to distinguish the political charges from the religious ones brought against Jesus. It is here that Jesus explains the term "King of the Jews" and the spiritual Kingdom he came to found. John gives a profound insight into the passion and death of Jesus, thus joining for us the Jesus of history and the Jesus of faith, as only one of the Twelve could do.

A Jewish Thinker. Unlike Luke, the author knows Palestine very well. He is every bit as Jewish as Matthew, for he sets out to prove that Jesus is the fulfillment of everything that the Jews hold dear. He points to the fact that Jesus is the fulfillment of the Scriptures (5:39-47) and of the whole sacrificial system. He is the new temple (Jn 2), Israel's bridegroom (Jn 3), and the fulfillment of all their feasts (Jn 5-10). Jesus is the new Moses (Jn 6, 10), the unrecognized Messiah (Jn 7-8), the Passover lamb, the sacrifice, the victim, the priest, and the altar. This type of exposition had to be aimed at convincing a Jewish audience that Jesus was their Messiah, their shepherd-king. Gentiles would require a different approach.

The argument that John represents a time when Christians were being thrown out of the synagogues does not add weight to a late date for the Gospel. Paul testifies to this same rejection in his writings, which come from the 50s and early 60s. Acts 17 onwards illustrates the Jews' hostility towards Paul's mission and the fact that both Paul and the Christians could no longer go to the synagogues. Acts, Paul, and John use the same expression for Jews hostile to Christianity—"The Jews"—thus differentiating between those who have gone over to Christ and those who resist Christianity.

From Jerome's comment above we can also see that Paul had to contend with the same heresies as John, and the spread of these false teachings led to Paul's wonderful exposition of the cosmic Christ in Colossians and Ephesians. The argument that John's Gospel was influenced by Gnostic writings has been knocked on the head by the recent discovery of a whole Gnostic library in Egypt. These writings are very different from those of John, and no influence could be accepted. John's writing has points of resemblance to the writings of the Qumran Community of the first century B.C., as can be seen from the Dead Sea Scrolls. In other words, John is a Jewish thinker and writer influenced by the events of his own country, during and after the time of Christ.

John alludes to the destruction of Jerusalem (Jn 11:48) as a future possibility, not a past event. The explanation given in 2:19-22 is that Jesus is the true temple, the place where God should be worshiped. Spiritually then, the events of A.D. 70 (in the future) are to be explained by the events of A.D. 30 (in the present). The destruction of the temple follows the death of Jesus, which opens access to God for Jews and Gentiles. If the fall of Jerusalem and the destruction of the temple had already occurred at the time of his writing, it seems probable that John would have referred to them as the fulfillment of prophecy.

Pictures of Jesus. We could call this Gospel "Behold your God," for John presents Jesus' divinity clearly throughout. Yet he succeeds in illustrating the humanity of Jesus in a very balanced way. For example, Jesus cries at the death of Lazarus (an eyewitness detail), just before raising him from the dead, the greatest sign to Israel of Jesus' divinity before his own Resurrection.

This Gospel is like a great art gallery in its presentation of many wonderful pictures of Jesus. He is the creative Word of God in the prologue. In chapter 2 he is the new temple. In 3 he is the divine teacher, while in 4 he is the divine missionary. Chapter 5 shows him as the divine physician, and 6 as the divine manna. In 7 he is the living water, and in 8 he is both defender of the weak and merciful judge. Chapter 9 shows him as the light of the world, and 10 as the divine shepherd. Chapter 11 presents Jesus as the conqueror of death, and 12 as the Messiah. In chapter 13 he is the humble servant of his brothers, and in 14 he is the Consoler of his church. Chapter 15 says that he is the vine, and 16 that he is the giver of the Holy Spirit. In chapter 17 we see the great intercessor, and in 18 the suffering servant of God. Chapter 19 shows us the uplifted savior, while 20 shows the risen victorious One. Lastly, chapter 21 illustrates him as the restorer of the penitent and guide for the mission to all the world.

These glorious pictures of Jesus had to be given by one who knew him personally and deeply, one who had contemplated the mystery of Christ for many years, one who decided to relate incidents not given by the other evangelists but still part of the tradition of the church.

Perhaps John had been more involved in these particular incidents than some of the other disciples? This is quite likely, for Jesus sent them out in pairs to evangelize during his own ministry. They were not always with him, nor all together. Neither Mark nor Luke was present during the ministry of Christ, and we do not have the original version of Matthew's Gospel. John, then, has the greatest authority to give us the ministry of Christ as it happened, for he was there the whole time.

JOHN'S LETTERS

The Fathers of the church credit John the Apostle with one letter as well as the Gospel. Two other letters under the name come from one who is called John the Elder. The letters are so like John's Gospel that they must at least come from the same "school" of thinking, if not from the same hand.

The first letter is the most important of the three. It is an encyclical letter to the churches, stressing the importance of faith and love in Christian living. It definitely carries the stamp of the beloved disciple.

The second letter is addressed to the "elect lady and her children," a designation for a local church. The third letter is an attempt to settle a dispute regarding leadership among the churches under John's authority.

THE BOOK OF REVELATION

The early church's testimony to the authorship of John the Apostle lies with Justin Martyr (A.D. 150), Irenaeus, the Muratorian Canon, Clement of Alexandria, Tertullian, Hippolytus, and Origen. Yet despite this abundance of testimony, modern scholars disagree. Critical examination of the text brings them to conclude that the fourth Gospel and the Apocalypse could not come from the same hand, at least in the final form of the text. This does not mean that the revelation it contains did not come from the Apostle, but that the final draft of the text was done by somebody else. Scholars still accept the traditional date for the composition of the book, that it was written during the persecution under Domition (A.D. 81-96). This, of course, coincides with the lifetime of John the Apostle.

The Apocalypse first includes letters to the churches of Asia, in which the spiritual condition of each one is revealed and a challenge is given to serve the Lord more faithfully. Then the author gives a series of prophetic visions: the seven seals (Rv 4-8); the seven trumpets (Rv 8-11); the seven bowls (Rv 15-19); and the visions of the last things (Rv 19-22). John speaks of a great struggle between good and evil that is now taking place and will continue to be played out in human history. It will reach its grand finale in the triumph of Christ.

Like the seven churches in John's day, all nations now and in the future are involved in this great drama. Each person and nation must make the decision for or against Christ. They may align themselves either with the great harlot or with the bride of the lamb; with the beast and his representatives or with Christ and his ambassadors.

During the struggle for world domination, many will

suffer for Christ, and many will be called to martyrdom. This is a privilege, for Jesus is the true King of Kings and Lord of Lords who will ultimately conquer and reign. Calling on his knowledge of the Old Testament and the prophets who went before him, John describes the glory of Heaven in an effort to call everyone to follow the Lamb wherever he goes.

Whether or not we understand John's imagery fully or follow his plot, or grasp the meaning of his plagues, we cannot fail to hear the ringing call to follow Christ. John encourages the church to stand up and witness for Christ during a time of persecution. He received his revelations while imprisoned on the Island of Patmos. His confinement gave him time to contemplate the effect of the Christ event on world history. Understanding the true meaning of the sacrificial death of Jesus on Calvary, John could see his ultimate triumph in the world. It is thus a very encouraging text, whether one is in a time of persecution or not.

It is significant that the Bible, which began with the drama of the choice between good and evil in the garden of Eden and the apparent triumph of evil, should end with the triumph of good over evil because of the victory of Jesus, the Second Adam, in the Easter garden of the Resurrection. All of us are called to participate in the struggle and in the victory of Christ.

Part V

The Problem of Truth

SEVENTEEN

The Gospels
Come under Attack

A S THE GOSPELS HAVE BEEN SUBJECTED to a barrage of textual
criticism in the past one hundred years, questions have
arisen concerning their veracity. These questions came
slowly at first, but now that the results of biblical criticism
have trickled down from the academics to the ordinary
person, the crisis of truth is upon us. Initially it was thought
almost blasphemous to question the Gospels, but all that
has changed. Now everyone is asking questions, and some
even query foundational doctrines of the Christian faith.
Although a flood of literature has appeared to demonstrate
one position or another of scholarship, the fundamental
questions of the faithful are the same.

Many people today are asking, Can we trust the Gospels
anymore? How do we know that what they say is true,
when even the scholars are questioning them? Are we
dealing with facts, or have we been duped? Are there not
voices claiming that Luke, for example, made up his infancy
stories? Why does Matthew's infancy narrative differ?
Surely Jesus' family was the only source of information.
Were the Magi real people? Was there a star over Bethlehem? How could Matthew know of Joseph's dreams? And
so on. There seems to be no end to what we need to verify.

159

THE CRITICS' STANCE

Before we begin this discussion, it may be necessary to state once again that the results that scientists can achieve are always limited by the instruments that they use. This may seem obvious, but we need to remember this with regard to literary analysis also. One can only achieve what the tools permit. The historico-critical exegesis of the Holy Scriptures reduces itself to an enquiry into the historical sources and to philological-literary analysis of the text. Or to put it in lay language, it limits itself to the study of the word, the sentence, the manner, the place, and the how of the instrument that God used to relate the Word of God to us.

This does not allow the scholar to touch the underlying mystery of the Word, which is a greater reality than the complex of words and sentences that expresses it. The danger of historico-critical analysis is that it can imprison the Word of God in its own methods, for it restricts the Scriptures to a merely historical or philological-grammatical framework. It is interested only in the material aspects of the texts, which it considers the only verifiable ones. This process can imprison the Holy Spirit!

Without the added dimension that places us before the mystery of the Word, first in the words of the book and then in the Word incarnate, scholars think they can bypass the mystical interpretations of the New Testament writers to reach "authentic Christianity" or even to find the "historical Jesus." They then proceed to measure this "Jesus" whom they find, and for many of them he does not "measure up" to the risen Lord at all. They paint a picture of a very ordinary Jesus before Calvary, one who may not have known from the beginning that he was God. (You and I are permitted to know who we are, but not Jesus.)

Some scholars seem to only accept the twentieth-century idea of history, a scientific data-based thing. This is foreign to ordinary people today, let alone to past generations. It is a rare human being who can relate even the simplest fact without interpretation. All our newspapers are colored by the national, political, and religious bias of the producers. All national history books are similarly biased. Even family and personal history is colored by the beliefs and convictions of the storyteller.

MISSING THE PEARL

How can we remove the interpretation of Jesus given to us by his own chosen witnesses, and hope to understand him? As Paul feared in writing to the Corinthians, we are in danger of producing a "new Jesus" or a "new gospel." One cannot reasonably expect a text that has withstood the test of time to play the history game by twentieth-century rules. History is related in the Scriptures by the rules understood in ancient times, and this we must respect. What these writers had to tell us was more than a chronological set of incidents, no matter how important they were.

To approach the Scriptures from such a dry intellectual framework deprives the researcher of the depth of God's Word, which comes to us from the Holy Spirit as well as from human authors. The Word will not yield its treasures to such analysis, necessary though it is. God reveals himself in the Scriptures through the Holy Spirit, at work in the reader as much as in the writer. In 1 Corinthians 2:11-13, Paul says that "nobody knows the qualities of God except the Spirit of God. Now the Spirit we have received is not the spirit of the world but God's own Spirit, so that we may understand the lavish gifts God has given us. And these are what we speak of, not in the terms learned from human philosophy, but in terms learned from the Spirit, fitting spiritual language to spiritual things."

One must therefore read the Bible on the level that it was written—that is, on the spiritual level. A text from the Gospel must be read in its proper context in order to be understood—its context in that Gospel and in the whole Bible.

To restore the Bible to its richness, one must accept the witnesses that God chose to impart and interpret the Scriptures for us. This is the living tradition of both Testaments; the community of believers under the Mosaic Covenant and the Christian church. The church gave us the New Testament, and the church alone can interpret it for us, especially in those areas where scholars have been unable to verify historical facts. We must remember that the Gospels were given to us by the church in the first one hundred years of its history, when the events it relates were fresh in people's minds. These early Christians felt no need to supply proof of what they taught.

READ IN THE SPIRIT

As the "Dogmatic Constitution on Divine Revelation" says (2.9): "Sacred Tradition and Sacred Scripture, then, are bound closely together, and communicate one with the other. For both of them, flowing from the same divine well-spring, come together in some fashion to form one thing and move towards the same goal. Sacred Scripture is the speech of God as it is put down in writing under the breath of the Holy Spirit. And Tradition transmits in its entirety the Word of God which has been entrusted to the Apostles by Christ the Lord and the Holy Spirit. It transmits it to the successors of the Apostles so that, enlightened by the Spirit of truth, they may faithfully preserve, expound, and spread it abroad by their teaching. Thus it comes about that the church does not draw her certainty about all revealed truths from the

Holy Scriptures alone. Hence both Scripture and Tradition must be accepted and honored with equal feelings of devotion and reverence."

The Gospels were not just given to us "in the letter" but also very much "in the Spirit." To understand them, therefore, they must be read in the Spirit. The final aim of exegesis must be the spiritual understanding of the Scriptures, in the light of the risen Christ. This was the angle from which the Bible was given to us by the first Christian witnesses, and this is what defines us as Christian readers.

We are into true theology when we seek what God is saying to his church today in the sacred Scriptures. True exegesis is *Fides quaerens intellectum*, which means that faith seeks understanding. So the seeker must approach the Word from the point of faith and love, for the inspired writers communicated the Word in the language of faith and love. This is therefore the way to "get on their wavelength" and truly hear them, as they testify to all that they have seen and heard. This is what the Vatican Council meant when it counseled us to read the Scriptures in the same spirit in which they were written. To refuse to do this is to have the Bible remain closed to us, even if we can write a literary analysis of every book in it.

EIGHTEEN

The Infancy Narratives: Fact or Fiction?

THE HISTORICITY of the infancy narratives is a much debated matter today among scholars. What are the issues involved?

TWO DIFFERENT STORIES

On reading the texts of Matthew and Luke we are struck by the differences between the two accounts. Each reflects on incidents that the other omits. Matthew speaks from Joseph's point of view, while Luke relates Mary's story. In Matthew's text the annunciation is to Joseph, while Luke describes the annunciation to Mary.

Matthew relates the story of the Magi, who were guided by a star and came bearing precious gifts to the newborn. This is followed by the flight into Egypt and the massacre of the innocents by Herod the Great. Finally there is the return to Israel with the family settling in Nazareth, followed by Jesus' thirty years of silence before his public ministry.

Luke omits all that and gives us the family history of John the Baptist, then that of Jesus. The annunciation to Mary is followed by her visit to Elizabeth. Luke sets Jesus' birth in the context of world history. The angels proclaim the birth from the heavens, prompting the shepherds to come and adore the baby. Mary and Joseph later present the child in the temple. Luke goes on to describe a scene from Jesus' youth, his finding in the temple at twelve years of age.

Many scholars today say that we cannot reconcile the accounts of Matthew and Luke, but the church has ordered the events into a possible chronology in the certainty that she is dealing with historical events. These facts are transmitted by tradition, orally and in writing. Each evangelist felt free to speak about those incidents he knew about or those he felt relevant to his purpose in writing his Gospel.

PUTTING THEM TOGETHER

There is a traditional way to put both accounts together: The angel announced to Zechariah in Jerusalem the birth of John the Baptist, and Elizabeth became pregnant. The annunciation to Mary in Nazareth came six months later. Since she did not tell Joseph, even though she was his betrothed, he was ignorant of the mystery initially. Mary went to help Elizabeth in the later stages of Elizabeth's pregnancy. Elizabeth was given a revelation regarding Mary's pregnancy and who Jesus was. Sometime later Joseph became aware of Mary's pregnancy and was very disturbed by it, even to the point of wanting to dissolve the marriage. The Lord intervened and announced the mystery to Joseph, who then accepted God's will for himself and his family. He completed the marriage arrangements immediately, so that he and Mary could begin life together.

Some months later a census demanded their presence in Bethlehem, Joseph's hometown as a descendant of David. There Jesus was born, and the angels announced his birth to the world. Shepherds received the message and were the first people to proclaim the birth of the Son of God. Mary and

Joseph stayed in Bethlehem for some months, maybe even a year, during which they took the child to the temple for Mary's purification and Jesus' presentation as the firstborn. During this time the Magi arrived, creating a stir in high places in Jerusalem. However, the Magi succeeded in visiting the child, offered their precious gifts, and went away without informing the authorities. Herod ordered the massacre of all male children under the age of two.

Joseph was warned in a dream to leave Israel at once, and the family left during the night for Egypt, where they stayed until after the death of Herod the Great in 4 B.C. Jesus must have been three years old when the family set out for Nazareth, where they settled. As a youth of twelve years, Jesus had to be presented to the priests in the temple in order to become "a son of the law." He entered into dispute with the teachers and stayed in the temple area for three days. When Mary and Joseph finally found him, he went back to Nazareth and silent obedience, until God's time arrived for his public mission.

We must not expect the scholars of critical analysis to accept this scenario, since they insist on verifying each point from the annals of history. We can not always have this proof in the case of ancient texts. So are we dealing with witnessed history or just a wonderful story? Or are these stories true in the sense of bearing a kernel of truth with additions that belong to interpretation?

There is no doubt that both Matthew and Luke are interpreting the facts for us. They do that by the literary structures they use. They also present their heroes in the light of the Old Testament "prophecy and fulfillment" framework. They cast their characters in Old Testament terms, so that we can see them through lenses that we understand.

The facts presented by both evangelists are the following: Jesus' mother, Mary of Nazareth, was a virgin at the time of the conception of Jesus, the Son of God. This virgin was betrothed to Joseph of Nazareth, but they had not begun to live together at that time (Mt 1:16-20; Lk 1:27, 34). Joseph was of the house of David; they do not tell us if Mary was also (Mt 1:16-20; Lk 1:27; 2:4-5). Both the conception and the coming birth of Jesus were announced by an angel (Mt 1:20-21; Lk 1:26-38).

Jesus was conceived by the Holy Spirit, and this unique intervention of God in human history constituted Jesus Son of God in a unique way, for he had no human father. He was fully human though, for he had a human mother (Mt 1:18-20; Lk 1:35). Joseph was not the father of Jesus, for he had nothing to do with his conception (Mt 1:18-25; Lk 1:34-35). The name Jesus was given by the angel before he was born (Mt 1:21; Lk 1:32). Jesus is the Savior, but not in any political sense, for he will save us from our sins (Mt 1:21; Lk 2:11). Jesus was born after Joseph and Mary went to live together (Mt 1:24-25; Lk 2:4-8). Jesus was born in Bethlehem (Mt 2:1; Lk 2:4-8, 15-20). Finally, Jesus grew up in Nazareth (Mt 2:22-23; Lk 2:39, 51).

MATTHEW AND JOSEPH

As we can see, the two accounts concur on all the major points of doctrine. The evangelists obtained their information from the teaching of the Apostles and the tradition, but we must remember that all the scattered communities of the early church may not have had all the details. Some stories may have been preserved in one area, some in another.

They would have been remembered in a particular context also. For instance, the Jewish audience of Matthew's Gospel were obviously asking a lot of questions regarding Joseph's role, and Matthew set out to answer them. It was a matter of debate among them as to who Jesus' father was (see Jn 5:18; 8:19, 25, 27, 58). This point was also vital for establishing Jesus as the Son of God.

While pointing out very clearly that Joseph was not the father of Jesus in the genetic sense, Matthew shows that he was not an "added extra" to the mystery. He was called by God to head the Holy Family and "father" Jesus in the emotional and social sense. Joseph would have had a formative role in Jesus' life and would have been a role model for the youth. It was no small matter to be the authority to whom the Son of God would submit. We can be grateful to Matthew for dealing with this, for he has given us an insight into God's ways and into the Holy Family.

Matthew points out that the bottom line for those who are chosen to cooperate with God's plans for the Redemption of the world is heroic obedience to the Word of God, no matter how God sends it. Heroic commitment to the will of God must be the rule of life. Joseph's humble submission to God's will and Word are revealed in Matthew 1:24-25; 2:14-15, 21-23. It was not Joseph's whim or personal ambition that ruled that household, but God's will. Mary's submission and obedience to God through Joseph are implied in all these texts (see also Lk 1:35-38; 2:1-8).

Obedience to God was costly for Mary and Joseph in personal terms. Until the truth of Jesus' origins would be known, the townspeople of Nazareth would only be aware of the irregularity of his birth, rather than the mystery of his birth for he was born too soon after Joseph and Mary came together. This naturally led to suspicion of Joseph, and of Mary as an adulteress. Accusations like this have been flung at them throughout history by those who reject the divinity of Christ and reject Christianity itself.

LUKE AND MARY

The Lukan community was fascinated by the fact that God chose a woman as his partner in Redemption. This gave women a status and role in the church that they did not enjoy under the old covenant. The Greek world wondered if it was even possible for a woman to be worthy to mother the Son of God. How could this happen, if she were the child of ordinary parents like the rest of us? This type of enquiry led Luke and his church to deal with the mystery from Mary's side, thus giving us newer insights than Matthew, who limited himself to the matter from Joseph's angle. The church benefits from the richness of two accounts that are more important together than separately.

To make his point Luke presented his subject in a series of scenes, like a play. He did this deliberately so that we could compare his main characters and learn from the contrasts he presented. For example, scene one has a priest, Zechariah, carrying out his normal duties in the temple, while the second scene has a young woman, Mary, at her normal duties at home in Nazareth, a long way from the temple and its privileges. The angel Gabriel visits both of them with a message about a miraculous birth. There are problems for both in the timing of the coming births: for Zechariah it is too late, and for Mary it is too early. He is too old, and she has not yet completed her marriage to Joseph. For both it seemed impossible from a human point of view. One might expect the priest to believe in the message of God and the young girl to have difficulty, but Mary believes and Zechariah doubts God's word.

Both Zechariah and Mary are told that they will have a son, who will be vital to God's plan for the salvation of the world. Both men will be great in God's sight, and prophets. One is the precursor, the other is the Savior. John's birth is miraculous in the sense that God overcame the old age of the parents and the barrenness of the mother. Jesus' birth is miraculous in an altogether higher sense, for it is impossible to human nature for a virgin to give birth. Jesus' birth is, therefore, an act of creation that is unique in the history of the world.

Luke has put his information together so as to highlight

what he wishes to say. He wants us to compare the conception of John the Baptist and that of Jesus. We are to conclude that although John was a great prophet, Jesus far exceeds him in importance. Luke contrasts the faith and submission of Zechariah and Mary in order to exalt the faith of Mary. The added scene of the Visitation highlights the greatness of Mary, while Zechariah goes into silence until God's word comes to pass.

Likewise Luke compares the birth, circumcision, and hidden life of John with that of Jesus. We note that in John's case the earth rejoices in the coming of a great prophet (see Zechariah's canticle, Lk 1:68-79), and the family celebrates a great intervention of God on their behalf. But in the case of Jesus, the heavens rejoice in the gift of the Savior to the world. The earth rejoices in the persons of the shepherds, who represent all those who will benefit from Jesus' salvation.

Luke places Jesus' birth in the context of world history, for Jesus is the Savior of all the world. Luke is interpreting Jesus and Mary for us; that is his role as teacher.

Luke is anxious for us to see the relative importance of John the Baptist vis-á-vis Jesus, a matter of great importance in the early church. The missionaries met disciples of John in their travels (see Acts 19:1-7), and there was considerable debate regarding the importance of John versus Jesus. It was the duty of the church to show the preeminence of Jesus, and Luke does this marvelously in the infancy narratives.

CRITICISMS AND THE CHURCH'S RESPONSES

These texts contain some very sensitive doctrines for Catholics, like the virgin birth and the implied perpetual virginity of Mary, for instance. Scholars run into difficulty when they cannot verify from outside sources statements found in these accounts. The problem is that the material in the infancy narratives is not referred to elsewhere in the New Testament. One would expect historians of the period to mention events like the census and the massacre of the infants. So far, scholars have not been able to verify the massacre from available sources. There is great debate regarding the census. Some scholars claim that it took place in A.D. 6 or 7 instead of B.C.!

The fact that these events cannot be verified by literary or archeological sources does not mean that they did not occur. It merely says that we lack proof, and more discoveries will have to be made. In the early part of this century scholars claimed that John's Gospel was not historically accurate because there was no pool with five porticos found in Jerusalem (Jn 5:2). Recent excavations to the northwest of the church of St. Anne in Jerusalem have revealed two enormous cisterns separated by a wall, which allows for the possibility of five porticos (four on a side plus one on the wall separating the cisterns); and excavations a little to the east of those cisterns have revealed grottoes which seem to have been used as a site of pagan healing rituals. All of this does make a plausible setting for the healing of John 5.

With regard to the Virgin Mary, critical scholars have a theory that the church gradually developed its understanding of both Jesus and Mary, and so the scriptural texts represent an earlier rather than later grasp of these realities. It seems that the Gospels developed the passion narratives first. The *Logia* or sayings of Jesus were simultaneously gathered and put in some order, and finally the infancy narratives developed. The high Christology of the infancy narratives would then represent a later development in theology in the church, rather than a pre-Calvary understanding of who Jesus was. The post-Resurrection understanding of Jesus is written into these narratives.

The church knew that Mary was a virgin and had remained a virgin all her life, though Scripture does not deal with the latter. The virginity of Mary says something about who Jesus is and where he came from. Though he had a human mother, his Father was, literally, God. It was up to the church, guided by the Holy Spirit, to look further into this mystery, which she has done in her Mariology. We respect her discernment on the matter.

From Ignatius of Antioch (A.D. 100) onwards, the Fathers of the first six centuries of the church speak extensively about Mary's virginity and her privilege as the Mother of God. They place her as the model for all Christians. The very earliest creeds of the church state that Jesus was "born of the Virgin Mary." Until the rationalists of the nineteenth century this was understood in the biological sense and was never questioned. It is fixed in the Christian consciousness and testified to by saints and mystics of all ages.

The virginal conception of Jesus is part of the official teaching of the church, which has the privilege from God to teach infallibly on all matters of faith and morals. Besides, the church has lived in the presence of Jesus for two thousand years, and she knows him to be both human and divine in the literal sense of those words. In John 14:26 Jesus promised that the Holy Spirit would always guide the church to the inner meaning of his teaching. Thus we can have faith that the church, or the living tradition, has told us the truth about the virginal conception of Jesus and the perpetual virginity of Mary. There is no need for sophisticated ways around these doctrines.

MAGI, STARS, AND ALL THAT!

Scholars have great difficulty in accepting Matthew's account of the Magi, the star, the massacre, and the flight into Egypt, the latter two because they cannot verify them from any known sources. Those with a rationalist bent have no time for the miraculous content of the narratives anyway, so they are automatically prejudiced against dreams and angelic appearances. They are inclined to put Matthew's account into the literary form of Midrash, that is, inspired commentary on Scripture. Some even say that Matthew's account is folkloric and imaginative, that he is rereading many Old Testament texts in the light of Christ. Therefore, the star would not be literal but literary.

These scholars attribute to Matthew an elaborate reconstruction of Old Testament texts. For example, he is said to "read" Joseph in the light of the patriarch Joseph in Genesis 37. Joseph, too, was a dreamer. He went down to Egypt as a result of persecution from his own people. The scholars say that the annunciation to Joseph is cast in the same mold as that concerning Isaac in Genesis 17 and Samuel in Judges 13. Jesus' escape from Herod's massacre bears resemblance to the escape of the baby Moses from the massacre ordered by Pharaoh in Exodus 1 and 2. They claim that the story of the Magi and the star comes from Numbers 22 to 24. This is the story of Balaam, a seer from the east, who saw "the star arise out of Jacob" but at a distance in time (Num 24:7, 17).

We do not doubt the Old Testament background to the narrative. How one interprets the evidence is important. Matthew has a "prophecy and fulfillment" theme running throughout his Gospel. Why would he change that in the infancy narratives? In fact, the whole New Testament reads the Old Testament in the light of Christ. Would we expect otherwise, when the Resurrection and Pentecost prove that Jesus is the fulfillment of the Scriptures? The evangelists saw that what was foretold in the Old Testament, sometimes in a very shadowy way, pointed to what happened in this greatest intervention of God in history.

Matthew cast his characters in Old Testament guise, for that is how his hearers would understand his salvific message. His Gospel is addressed to a people who were steeped in the Old Testament and who would expect an unbroken line in the history of salvation. They already knew that earlier figures in the Old Testament pointed to later ones, so Matthew's reading of these New Testament characters would fall into the same line of thinking. He was a Jew speaking to Jews about Jews.

THE GOSPEL IN MINIATURE

In the story of the Magi and the star, Matthew is dealing with the proclamation of the coming of the Savior to the world. Who would announce Jesus to the world, and who would receive him? One would expect the Jewish nation to announce him, steeped as it was in the Old Testament prophecies about the Messiah, and the Gentile world to reject him as just a local figure for the Jews. The opposite happened. The Jewish political and religious leaders—represented here by Herod, the chief priests, and the scribes—rejected him and brought about his death, and eventually the deaths of many of his immediate followers. The Gospels illustrate that those associated with Jesus, either in his origin or his triumph, would suffer the hatred and rejection of the world, and many would be martyred. The massacre of the innocents is a prophetic forecast of the destiny of the saints throughout history, as the battle between God and the world powers is fought to its conclusion.

If we are surprised by the rejection of the Jews, we are taken aback even more that the Gentiles, here represented by the Magi, sought and found him. People of good will were guided by God to seek salvation. This is the meaning of the star, a symbol of divine providence, which guides our lives when we allow it. Divine providence is a gentle but exact guide, just as the star was. Those who follow the leading of the Holy Spirit will not lose their way. They will be brought gently but firmly into the whole mystery of God against all odds, just as the Magi were led into the presence of Jesus, Mary, and Joseph.

Just as the Magi found that Jesus was indeed the Savior,

that Mary was his real mother, and that Jesus was reared in a normal family, so will all other seekers of truth. The Magi's response to the mystery was to honor the family. The treasures they offered reveal Jesus' royalty (gold), divinity (frankincense), and coming suffering (myrrh). These gifts also speak of the transformation that comes to those who allow Jesus to be their Savior. They are freed of the slavery to money (gold) to live as sons and daughters of God (frankincense). They too will suffer, and it will be redemptive suffering for themselves and others (myrrh).

The Gentiles had very little help in their search, just their natural knowledge of astronomy. But their hearts sought truth, and as Jesus later taught, "Everyone who asks receives; everyone who searches finds; everyone who knocks will have the door opened" (Mt 7:8; see also Rom 1:19-20; 2:14-15). Matthew wants to say that only the wise seek God, but those who seek him always find him.

The Gentiles eventually discovered that the Savior of the world was also the King of the Jews, and they went to the Jewish Scriptures to learn how to interpret him. In the early church Jewish men like Matthew taught them about Jesus. This is foreseen in the story of the Magi, who sought those who knew the Scriptures, to help them determine where to find the Messiah. They knew that the ultimate secret of Jesus' identity was locked up in the special revelation of God to Israel (Mt 2:2-6).

Matthew points out the paradox that while the Jews could explain Jesus, they did not come to worship him as a nation. They instead conspired to kill him. But the Gentiles worshiped the King of the Jews, both in his infancy and after his triumph. After his death Jesus returned to lead his people to salvation, and no worldly power could stop him. In the same way, he escaped death in childhood and returned to Israel to bring God's will to completion in Redemption.

Here we can see that not only is Matthew's infancy narrative "gospel" in the sense of being the good news of salvation, but it is also the gospel in miniature. God did indeed make himself present to us in Jesus. The mystery of human acceptance and rejection of the Savior is still played out in history. There are still those who are far off, who have never heard the message, but whose hearts are good. Because they seek the truth, God guides them to salvation in Christ. These are the wise ones who learn that God's merciful providence governs all who love him.

NINETEEN

The Bodily Resurrection of Jesus

BOTH ENDS OF THE GOSPEL have been subjected to scrutiny in this century. Critics question the bodily resurrection of Jesus, just as they question the virginal conception. These issues are connected, for they both touch on the nature of Jesus Christ.

We have come full circle: The Jews in Jesus' day continuously questioned him regarding who he *really* was, and the debate continued in the early church. Christians today are asking these questions, and some are seriously questioning the plausibility of a bodily resurrection. Theologians speak of some sort of "spiritual survival" after death that may not have involved a bodily resurrection. This sounds as if the body of Jesus may have rotted in its tomb. Since this is a contradiction of the term "resurrection," we need to reexamine the evidence.

AN AMAZING STORY

Jesus of Nazareth was crucified at Passover in the year A.D. 30, under Pontius Pilate, who was the Prefect of Judea (this title has been found on an inscription in Caesarea). Shortly afterwards, a dynamic religious movement appeared whose adherents claimed that their Master was alive, living among them as their Lord. This claim was so preposterous that either it was true or it proved the mass delusion of his followers. Yet this was the central teaching of the new church. They had the works to show as well as the words. They worked miracles just as Jesus had done, and lived a life of poverty and holiness in imitation of him.

Further, it soon became apparent that persecution would not silence them, for they were prepared to stake their lives on the truth of what they taught. This was demonstrated in the martyrdom of Stephen by the Sanhedrin in A.D. 32, and of the Apostle James by Herod Agrippa in A.D. 44.

What is more, the new church spread like wildfire, with many of the Jewish priests joining it (Acts 6:7). There were mass conversions among the people also (Acts 2:41; 4:4; 5:14), many of whom would have known Jesus in his lifetime, since he had traveled the length and breadth of the land during his ministry. Within a short time the new church had spread to all the surrounding countries through people who were in Jerusalem for Pentecost (Acts 2). This message of the Resurrection of the crucified One created churches everywhere, whereas one would have expected it to create laughter and scorn (Acts 17:32). Very soon the movement reached the palace of Caesar himself, through his own army (Phil 1:13-14). It became such a threat to the empire that it aroused persecution.

Obviously something had happened, and it was dynamite to anyone who heard it. A vague theory of survival after death would not have been news to anyone conversant with the Old Testament, for the psalmists struggled with this idea long before the knowledge of eternal life was revealed to Israel. Later, in the second century B.C., the prophet Daniel revealed that there was life after death, both for the good and the wicked (Dn 12:2). The Book of Wisdom corroborated this (Wis 3:1-12), and Psalm 16:9-11 says: "My body too will rest secure, for you will not abandon me to Sheol, you cannot allow your faithful servant to see the abyss.'' Belief in the immortality of the soul and belief in ghosts and spirits were widespread throughout the Greco-Roman world. If life after death was all that the Apostles had to say, then they were not announcing anything new or powerful to their generation.

In fact, what the Apostles said was very disturbing, for they claimed that their beloved Master was risen from the dead by God, his Father, on the third day after a cruel death by torture. What is more, he still bore the marks of his passion on his glorified body! This was bodily resurrection all right, take it or leave it. And they never changed their story, not even under torture. Peter, the main witness, was eventually crucified, considering it a privilege to die like Jesus. It apparently did not occur to him to save his life by denying that the Resurrection had ever happened. Instead he died to witness to its truth. Paul, the other major witness of the New Testament, died for the same truth.

If there is one thing that can be said to be at the very heart of Christianity, it is the bodily resurrection of Jesus of Nazareth, our Savior. Paul so rightly said in 1 Corinthians 15:14 that "if Christ has not been raised, then our preaching is without substance, and so is your faith." Christianity collapses if there is no Resurrection of Jesus, for its uniqueness hinges on it. To question the Resurrection, then, is to question our very existence as a church. If it is not true, then, as Paul says in 1 Corinthians 15:18, "we are of all people the most to be pitied, for we are deluded."

Yet a claim to bodily resurrection must be the most extraordinary statement that anyone can make. It raises many questions even for believers who want to understand. The rationalists are in trouble though, for they do not permit the miraculous, and with the Resurrection of Jesus the idea of miracle enters a new realm. So we must not be surprised at either disbelief or questioning, for questions regarding the Resurrection are as old as Christianity itself.

THE EMPTY TOMB

This was the first piece of evidence that confronted the disciples on Easter day. The tomb was empty, but the grave cloths were there. What were they to make of this information?

Several conclusions could be drawn, and it is not good enough for scholars to dismiss the empty tomb as a later "invention" of the evangelists to counteract the docetic heresy, (which denied that Jesus had a real body and claimed that he only seemed to suffer and die on the cross). It would be impossible to imagine how the story of the Resurrection would have been accepted if the body of Jesus were still in the tomb! The very first message that the Apostles received was that the body was gone (Jn 20:2), and its disappearance had to be explained.

It was only later when they were preaching the Resurrection, and it was obvious that anyone could visit the tomb for themselves, that the stress on the empty tomb was given. The doctrine of a resurrection was impossible if the tomb was *not* empty. So the disappearance of the body is crucial. What happened to it?

One of the earliest and most persistent rumors was that someone had stolen the body. The Gospels hint at this in John 20:15-16, where Mary of Magdala mistakes Jesus for the gardener and asks him whether he stole the body. The disciples too thought grave robbers might be responsible, for they treated the message of the women that Jesus was alive as "pure nonsense" (Lk 24:11; Mk 16:11). This legend persisted even into the time of Tertullian in the second century.

But who would want the body of a crucified man, who according to the Jewish law was accursed (Dt 21:23; Gal 3:13)? And why would they want it so soon after death? There were only three groups who might be interested in the body of Jesus: the Jewish leaders, the Romans, and the Apostles.

The Jewish leaders would not have stolen the body, since they had gone to such trouble to kill Jesus and to have his tomb sealed. They had remembered Jesus' prophecy regarding his rising on the third day, while the Apostles had forgotten it (Mt 27:62-66). They placed a guard at the tomb to squash the idea of a Resurrection. Their interest was in keeping the body of Jesus just where it was. They were also very anxious to squash the new movement of Christianity. If they had the body, they could have produced it to disprove the Resurrection.

The Jewish leaders visited the tomb, and they, too, found it empty. Matthew 28 says that they bribed the guards to say that the Apostles had come and stolen the body while they slept. These may not have been Roman guards (Mt 27:65; see Lk 22:4; Jn 18:3), for it would have been a capital offense to sleep on duty or to let their prisoner free (see Acts 12:19). Also, a Roman guard would have reported back to Pilate, not to the chief priests (Mt 28:11), that Jesus was risen from the dead. It would be strange for a Roman guard to work so closely with the chief priests when they were at enmity over the crucifixion of Jesus.

If it was indeed a Jewish guard, then the risen Lord himself sent a message to the priests that neither they, nor their seal on the tomb, nor their guard had power to keep him imprisoned in death, for he was the Lord of life (Rv 1:17). Rather than accept the truth of Jesus' Resurrection and its implications, the Jewish leaders chose to spread a lie, even though it made a laughingstock of them and their guard.

NO ONE FOUND THE BODY

If the story of the empty tomb was invented by the evangelists to strengthen the Resurrection claim, then it is strange indeed that the guards would report that it happened "while we slept." The information would only be of use to Christians if the guards had stayed awake and witnessed something! No, this report has a ring of truth to it. The chief priests must have believed it too, for they were willing to pay the guards to keep quiet. If it were merely a story about failure on duty, the guards would have been punished. Instead they agreed to become accomplices to the lie.

It is interesting to note that in all the Resurrection controversies of the first two centuries of the Christian era, no one was ever able to produce a body (or skeleton). During all this time the empty tomb kept its silent witness to the unbelieving and astounded world.

The Romans, too, had a vested interest in squashing Christianity. They did not want a new religious group stirring up trouble in an already troublesome region. If they had a body to produce to squash the rumors of Resurrection, they would have done it.

The bodies of executed criminals were considered the property of Rome, and they were thrown into a common grave at the crucifixion site. Archeology has uncovered the bones of a young crucified man in an ossuary in a rock-cut tomb in Jerusalem, dating between A.D. 7 and 20, showing that the Roman authorities could be lenient towards family sensibilities. In Jesus' case, Joseph of Arimathea, who was one of the Jewish Council and therefore one of the Jewish national leaders, requested the body of Jesus from Pilate. Because Pilate surrendered the body, it was no longer Roman property, and Joseph could bury it in the normal Jewish way.

An interesting discovery was made in Nazareth, Jesus' hometown. Archeology has uncovered an inscription probably from the time of Tiberias (A.D. 14-38). The emperor expresses his displeasure at reports regarding the removal of dead bodies from their graves. He warns that if this continues, the grave robbers will face the death penalty. Presumably Pilate would have accepted the story of the chief priests, and he would have reported that the body of Jesus had been stolen.

The Apostles are the next suspects for stealing the body of Jesus. Surely they would have a vested interest in a Resurrection story. The Jewish leaders set up the rumor regarding the Apostles. However, the Gospels make it clear that the Apostles were utterly shattered by the passion and death of Jesus. They panicked and fled at the first sign of Jesus' impending suffering and eventual death, beginning in Gethsemane. John was the only one present for the passion. The Apostles thought that their wonderful dream was all over, and they were "in mourning and in tears" (Mk 16:10). They were not expecting a Resurrection, and would not believe the story even when told by several different witnesses.

THE WOMEN'S STORY

The events become complicated at this point simply because the Resurrection of Jesus is the most earthshaking event that has ever occurred, and it left everyone stunned. The disciples may not even have tried to piece things together until a later point, when Christians wanted to know everything in detail. Even their final stories are confused!

It seems that a group of women—whether they went in one or two groups is not clear—went to the tomb on Easter morning. It was permitted to visit the tomb for three days after a death. Some of them thought they could enter the tomb to anoint the body of Jesus. Either they did not know of the guard or they thought that a Jewish guard would understand.

When they arrived the tomb was open, and the body of Jesus was missing. They were met by an unknown person—variously called "a young man," an angel, or angels—and he explained the mystery to the women. Jesus was not there, because he had risen from the dead. This was the astounding reality that explained the empty tomb. The empty tomb by itself could not reveal this; it could only be an added proof when the mystery was already known. Since this knowledge lay only with God, he had to reveal it through his ministering angel.

The women were told not to look among the dead for the Living One (Lk 24:5), and they were reminded of Jesus' prophecies regarding his passion and Resurrection. Matthew 28:6 puts it simply: "He is not here, for he has risen, as he said he would." And the church has sung it for twenty centuries: *Resurrexit sicut dixit, Alleluia!*

There appears to have been two reactions among the women: the first was fear and dread. Mark says that they fled, terrified, and told no one. That reaction was only for a time obviously, for Matthew 28 and Luke 24 say that they eventually told the disciples. Mary of Magdala, the fearless one, either alone or accompanied, went to tell Peter and John, who ran to investigate the empty tomb (Jn 20).

It is unreasonable to expect that these dramatic moments would have been remembered in every detail. Does it matter whether the women came to the tomb before daybreak or just after it? Whatever time they arrived they were late, for the Resurrection had already occurred, and God reserved its privacy for himself. It was only the results of the Resurrection that they could witness to.

The Apostles were in no mood for the women's story, which they took to be "pure nonsense" (Lk 24:11). Mark says that they were obstinately incredulous (16:14). Thomas did not believe even on the evidence of the other Apostles (Jn 20).

We cannot accuse the Apostles of being psychologically prepared for a Resurrection. An empty tomb was one thing, but a Resurrection was altogether another. (Modern theologians apparently agree!) They investigated the tomb, as you may be sure the Jewish and Roman authorities would have done also. None of the suspects knew what had happened to the body, and they all had a problem with that.

The only explanations so far were those of the guards and

the women, who did not communicate, who represented different sides of the problem, but whose stories concurred. Both groups claimed that the reason for the empty tomb was that Jesus was risen from the dead. But so far no one had seen him (Lk 24:24).

At this point the story almost reads like a modern "Whodunnit." All the suspects look completely innocent but are at the same time being accused by everybody else! But nobody can produce a body. It is gone. If neither friend nor foe has stolen the body, then the stupendous fact of a bodily resurrection stares us in the face.

After the Apostles came to believe in the Resurrection of Jesus, they did not venerate the tomb. It was common practice in Palestine at that time to venerate the tombs of holy men, like that of David in Jerusalem and Abraham in Hebron. But the tomb of Jesus had nothing in it! What would be the point of venerating stones? The Christians worshiped the risen Lord, the Living One (Rv 1:17-18), who dwelt as Savior in the heart of the converted sinner (Jn 14-16).

Jesus was also present in the blessed Eucharist (Jn 6; Lk 22; Mt 26; Mk 14), in their gatherings (Mt 18:20; 28:20), and in their mission to all the world (Mk 16:7, 20; Mt 28:18-20). Since he was with them, there was no need for the tomb. The angel of the Resurrection had guided them away from the tomb towards the living community, which was the extension of Jesus' incarnation. It is *there* that they would "see" him, meaning that their encounter with him would be in faith, but nonetheless real for all that (Lk 24:31-35).

THE BURIAL CLOTHS OF JESUS

The presence of the burial cloths in the tomb of Jesus was very significant. It is the oldest explanation given by the church for the fact that the body of Jesus was not stolen, for grave robbers would never strip a body and walk off with a stiff naked corpse in their hands. They would need extra wrappings to cover up their foul deed.

Here we can make an important comparison between the raising of Lazarus and that of Jesus. John says specifically that when Lazarus was raised, he came forth with the grave cloths still on him: "The dead man came out, his feet and hands bound with strips of material, and a cloth over his face. Jesus said to them, 'Unbind him, and let him go free' " (Jn 11:43-44).

Lazarus was brought back to *mortal life,* whereas Jesus was raised to a life that transcended everything mortal and material. Jesus left his tomb with a glorified body, whereas Lazarus left his with a resuscitated and healed body. Lazarus was still bound to time and space and still subject to sickness and death, whereas Jesus was the firstborn from the dead, utterly free from every limitation (Col 1:18). Neither need, sickness, nor death could ever touch him again. Jesus' body was completely transformed, although it still carried the marks of the crucifixion, like identification tags. He did not need the grave cloths of earth, for he was clothed in glory.

Since the raising of Lazarus was a preparation for the raising of Jesus and a great help to understanding it, let us look at a comparison between the two here. Both happened on the third day (Jn 11:7; 20:1). Jesus said that "this sickness will not *end in death, but it is for God's glory so that through it the Son of God may be glorified"* (emphasis mine). The crucifixion of Jesus would not end in death either, but in God's glory being revealed in the Resurrection, which in turn revealed the glory of Jesus, his Son. Jesus deliberately delayed until God's time to act for Lazarus. According to our reckoning of time, Jesus was too late, because Lazarus died. Jesus did not die until it was *his hour* in God's time also (Jn 11:9-10).

Martha and Mary, both disciples of Jesus, grieved deeply over Lazarus's death, and did not understand Jesus' action in allowing Lazarus to die. In the same way the Apostles and disciples grieved over Jesus' death without understanding the divine import of the event (Mk 16:10). Jesus himself grieved over the death of Lazarus, just as he grieved deeply over his own, in Gethsemane. In both cases he faced death as the ultimate punishment of the human race for its sinfulness. He contemplated the destructive power of sin as the ultimate cause of sickness, death, and Hell. He alone could transform the situation, but at great cost to himself. So contemplation of the tomb of Lazarus for him meant contemplating his own tomb.

Both Martha and Mary were able to believe in the resurrection of the body on the last day (Dn 12:2), but could not believe in a bodily resurrection in the here-and-now (Jn 11:25, 39). That would represent a great intervention of God of the type that disturbs us, and it is easier to shut out the possibility. Martha and Mary represent all disciples both then and now, who balk at the idea of bodily resurrection.

Jesus' reply to them was that victory over death lay within his power, for Lazarus, himself, and all those who believed in him: "I am the resurrection. Anyone who believes in me, even though that person dies, will live, and whoever lives and believes in me will never die." Just as Martha and Mary needed Jesus' help to understand the resurrection then, so the Apostles needed his help after his own Resurrection. He stayed with them for a period of forty days to instruct them.

In both resurrections there was a tomb and a stone rolled back. Lazarus was raised by Jesus, for it is Jesus' privilege to raise both the spiritually dead now and the physically dead on the last day (Jn 5:25-30). God the Father raised Jesus from the dead (Acts 2:23-24). The raising of Lazarus was a sign of Jesus' love for him in the immediate, and for all of us in promise (Jn 11:5, 37). Jesus' Resurrection is the sign of his love for the whole human race (Jn 13:1). Clearly the author of the fourth Gospel is trying to tell us that we can understand the wonder and message of Jesus' Resurrection by comparing it with that of Lazarus, his friend. And the raising of Lazarus was a bodily affair that created a great stir in Jerusalem, just as the Resurrection of Jesus did.

JESUS REVEALS HIMSELF

The rationalists and unbelievers make a case against the Resurrection because the Gospel accounts differ so much. But these differences are an argument in favor of the Resurrection rather than against it. If the early church had been afraid of such discrepancies raising doubts, they could have tried to "tidy up" the accounts.

People who witness a major earthquake, for example, are deeply affected and will remember for several years the main events, but over time their recollections of exact details may become less clear. This is exactly what we have in the Resurrection accounts. The witnesses are clear on the main events, but not on details. The witnesses testify (1) that Jesus was crucified on a Friday and hastily buried; (2) that they all rested on the Sabbath; (3) that on the Sunday morning (before, at, or after dawn) the women went to the tomb, either to mourn or to anoint the body of Jesus; (4) that the leader of the group was Mary of Magdala; (5) that they found the tomb open and empty; (6) that an angel or angels told them that Jesus was alive, and they were to inform Peter and the others; (6) that Mary of Magdala told Peter and John, and the other women reported later; (7) that Peter and John investigated the empty tomb; (8) that John was the first Apostle to believe in the Resurrection; (9) that Jesus appeared first to the women, then to the disciples on the Emmaus road, then to the Apostles—ten of them in John's Gospel, and all in the other Gospels—then in Galilee (Jn 21), and finally at his Ascension; (10) that during this time Jesus instructed his Apostles and disciples, explaining the Scriptures in the light of the Resurrection (Lk 24); (11) that he commanded them to begin the mission to all the world in his name.

Even reading the Gospels we get the impression that they have not told everything that happened. This is confirmed by other New Testament witnesses: for example, Acts 1:3 says, "He had shown himself alive to them by many demonstrations: for forty days *he had continued to appear to them* and tell them about the Kingdom of God" (emphasis mine).

Luke is here saying that the evangelists (and he was one of them) selected from a vast amount of testimony to illustrate only some things regarding the Resurrection. John says the same in John 20:30-31. Paul adds in 1 Corinthians 15:5-7 that Jesus "appeared to Cephas [Luke also has this in 24:35]; and later to the Twelve [this must be after the election of Matthias in Acts 1:26]; and next he appeared to more than five hundred of the brothers at the same time, most of whom are still with us [A.D. in 57], though some have fallen asleep; then he appeared to James, and then to all the Apostles. Last of all he appeared to me too." Clearly the Gospels did not set out to tell us everything, nor to give us a flat, two-dimensional picture. The events of the Resurrection were too dynamic and glorious for the witnesses to be restricted to any single point of view.

THE LIVING JESUS

The Christians' understanding of the Resurrection did not come from the empty tomb but from the glorious presence of the risen Jesus in their midst. Luke says that Jesus taught them for forty days after the Resurrection. It is obvious from Luke 24:27, 44 that they were given a Christological understanding of the Old Testament in terms of prophecy and fulfillment. Therefore, when they went out to preach the Resurrection, they did not preach the empty tomb but the Living One, whom they had experienced.

Each of the Gospels emphasizes the uniqueness of the Resurrection appearances. The evangelists go out of their way to say that the Apostles did not see a "vision." Jesus was really there, though his body was transformed in glory and hence not immediately recognized.

Mary of Magdala was able to cling to his feet (Jn 20:17). He walked to Emmaus with two of the men (Lk 24:1-35). He ate and drank with his Apostles (Lk 24:42). They were able to touch him (Lk 24:39) and examine his wounds (Jn 20:20, 27). He made breakfast for them by the Sea of Tiberias (Jn 21). He visited them often and instructed them for their new mission to all the world. He was seen by five hundred people at the same time (1 Cor 15:6). Even Paul, the only other person to claim a Resurrection appearance, says that it was different from the visions and revelations he had later. Paul was a man with profound spiritual experience, deep theological discernment, and a penetrating intellect, and he would know what he was talking about (1 Cor 15:8; 2 Cor 12:1-10).

The transformation that Jesus' presence brought about in the disciples was the greatest witness to those who were not privy to the Resurrection appearances. It was clear to observers that the mantle of Jesus had fallen upon the Apostles, and that they were continuing his mission to preach, teach, and work miracles in his name. To put it simply, the bodily Resurrection of Jesus had brought about a miraculous spiritual resurrection in the disciples. The church had risen from the death of unbelief, misunderstanding of Jesus' mission, and of Jesus himself to realize that they were one body with him and the extension of his incarnation in the world. The branches of the vine had the same life as the vine itself, so it could produce the same works to the glory of the Father. They soon learned that this identification with Jesus also meant that the church would suffer the passion, death, and glory of its Master and Lord. The physical body of Jesus was replaced by his mystical body, the church.

MODERN SKEPTICISM

Since the idea of a man resurrected from death into an entirely new level of existence—resurrection life—is so unique a claim, we can expect a host of objections. The simplest one is just that "when you're dead, you're dead!" Resurrection is a scientific impossibility, and the rationalists are impatient with the miraculous, which they see as childish and primitive. Yet our scientific age has had to face up to its abysmal ignorance of the universe in general. A new world of knowledge opened up in the twentieth century which should make us humble in the face of all that we do *not* know. Yet it can only produce a "big bang" theory for the origin of our world, and a theory of evolution for our origins. We are a generation that lives on theories, those of the scientists as well as those of the theologians. We need to remember that a theory is an unproven explanation of reality.

Real scientists know that they must examine the facts, especially when they do not understand them. Hence the research being done by scholars and theologians into the Resurrection is valid. They must ask the questions if we are to come to a deeper understanding eventually. But we need to avoid the trap that Paul warned us about in 1 Timothy 6:3-4, where we just want to argue and question everything without a good purpose.

As a result of questioning by scholars today, we are hearing that the Resurrection may not be "an historical event." Some say that we cannot know what happened on Easter day, for no one witnessed it. All we have is the Easter faith of the disciples, and this is as far as historical criticism can go. This makes the critics uncomfortable, for they can't "prove" the Resurrection from their research. Some want to say that Jesus survived death in some special way that is transhistorical. A spiritual survival after death, for a good man especially, would not have disturbed the Greeks, but they scoffed at the idea of a bodily resurrection. Neither would the idea of spiritual survival have turned Paul into the fiery missionary he became when Jesus revealed to him his victory over death.

Paul was already answering queries like this in 2 Timothy 2:16-18, where he told the young bishop to "have nothing to do with godless philosophical discussions—they only lead further and further away from true religion. Talk like this spreads corruption like gangrene, as in the case of Hymenaeus and Philetus, the men who have gone astray from the truth, claiming that the resurrection has already taken place. They are upsetting some people's faith." These men were most likely giving a completely spiritual explanation of the Resurrection of Jesus, as they did with the resurrection of the body of Christians on the last day. As Gnostics, they rejected the body as evil. Paul stoutly defends the corporeal nature of our salvation. Both Jesus' Resurrection and our future resurrection of the body are certain.

We are not left without guidance, however, for the living tradition of the church has given us an unbroken testimony to the bodily Resurrection of Jesus Christ. She has never wavered in this teaching in two thousand years. Catholic teaching does not permit us to believe that the body of Jesus corrupted in the tomb. The church fathers throughout the centuries have contemplated this mystery and written about it. The church firmly believes that the bodily Resurrection of Jesus is the essential forerunner to the eventual resurrection of all the dead (see 1 Thes 4:14).

Part VI

Ultimate Realities

TWENTY

Is There a Hell?

WHILE SCHOLARS AND THEOLOGIANS are questioning the historicity of the infancy and Resurrection narratives, Western society in general has called into question the teaching of the New Testament on sin and judgment. To a large extent society has simply put the moral teaching of Christ aside. We hear frequently that God is *so good* that there *could not* be a Hell. Or we hear that God is *so merciful* that "of course" everyone will be saved, regardless of their personal conduct.

So we are faced with a new set of problems. Can we trust the New Testament in what it teaches about sin and judgment? Does Hell really exist? Will there *really* be a Day of Reckoning? Or is this hellfire and brimstone just the language that preachers use to make us live a good life?

Let us begin by saying that the amount of teaching on sin and judgment is such that if we deny it, we reject at least half of the Gospels, to say nothing of the rest of the New Testament. This rejection leaves us with a mediocre presentation of Christ. This "nice" Jesus tells everyone to love one another, without any morality in that loving, because he accepts us as we are. This amounts to saying that Jesus would agree to the moral breakdown of society and family and all their attendant evils.

This is definitely not the Jesus of the Gospels, who lived a heroic life of holiness himself and demanded the same of everyone who followed him. Jesus made great moral demands, even on great sinners, and expected them to be lived out. The "gentle Jesus, meek and mild" is a travesty of the One who stirred Israel to the point of killing him, for he uncovered their sinful rejection of God's will and Word.

INFINITE MERCY

There is no doubt that God is infinitely merciful, in an utterly unfathomable way. He is also infinitely good and gracious, and his attitude towards all of us is love, as Psalm 145 points out. But this does not cancel Jesus' teaching that God is a moral God, who expects us to live lives worthy of his love and grace. The Gospels show Jesus' acceptance of prostitutes and sinners, but he did not leave them that way. He brought them through a thorough repentance of life, gave them God's loving forgiveness of their past, and demanded that they live an altogether new life. Examples of this are Mary of Magdala, Matthew the Apostle and Zaccheus, the chief tax collector of Jericho. These public sinners met Jesus and had their lives transformed by him. Each went on to live a life of exceptional holiness and service to humanity, in imitation of their beloved Master who had saved them.

There is no hint in the Gospels that Jesus' acceptance of sinners meant that they could go on sinning! His words to the adulteress in John 8:11 were, "Go away, and from this moment sin no more." Regarding the sinful woman in Luke 7:47 Jesus said, "For this reason I tell you that her sins, many as they are, have been forgiven her, because she has shown such love." Nowhere are we told that we can go on living immoral lives because God loves us *anyway*. Instead, we are told that although God loves us enough to send his *only Son* to save us, he (i.e., infinite love) expects us to respond to

Jesus' saving work with radical repentance (Jn 3:16-20).

When preaching stresses the joys of friendship with Christ and refuses to deal with responsibility and judgment, people find the Gospel not worth reading. They hear that they are okay as they are. There is no call to repentance, nothing to stir them to seek God (Hos 10:12). Hence many seminars today look into the question of whether the Gospels are even relevant to the twentieth century!

The Gospels, on the other hand, stress that persisting in sin has both short-term and long-term consequences. Our "eating, drinking, and making merry" affects our health, family relationships, work, and society. In the end we may face judgment for our refusal to accept God's grace and repent (Lk 12:16-21).

CHANGE YOUR WAYS

John the Baptist prepared the way for Jesus by preaching a radical repentance of life. The word used for repentance is *metanoia*, which means such a radical change in one's way of thinking about life that the former ways are put aside completely and one begins all over again. There is indeed "the old life" and "the new life" (2 Cor 5:17; Eph 4:24; Col 3:10). John warned the people that if they persisted in immorality, judgment awaited them, because God holds us responsible for our decisions and actions (Mt 3:2-12). They were told to produce the fruit of repentance in a holy life (Mt 3:9). People responded to this challenge by changing their lives.

THE DEMANDS OF JESUS

Jesus took up exactly the same message of repentance. If the Kingdom of God is to find a place in our lives, then the kingdom of darkness has to go, for the Spirit of God will not cohabit a place or person with the evil spirit (Mt 4:17). When sinners responded to Jesus, he showed his love and acceptance of them by forgiving them (Mk 2:9; Lk 7:48), by casting out evil spirits (Mk 4:24), and by curing the effects of sin and sickness. Jesus did not condone their sins (Jn 8:11), but he forgave sinners and offered them the chance to live as sons and daughters of God.

Jesus demanded a radical new morality from his followers. He interpreted the Ten Commandments more strictly than did Moses or the rabbis, and he raised them to a new level. For instance, he stated that the fifth commandment forbids not only killing but also the anger hidden in the heart that caused the killing (Mt 5:21-23). Enemies were to reconcile with one another (Mt 5:23-25). He pointed out that, according to the law of the Gospel, one could be guilty of far less than murder and still be in danger of Hell (Mt 5:21)!

The sixth commandment not only forbade adultery but also lust (Mt 5:27-30). Further, he taught that to remarry while one's previous partner still lived was another form of adultery (Mt 19:9). He demanded integrity in one's dealings and said that we should put up with life's hard knocks without retaliating (Mt 5:32-42). Everyone would be judged according to the way that he had judged his neighbor (Mt 7:1-5). Jesus' hardest demand of all was that we should love our enemies (Mt 5:43-48; Lk 6:27-29). His followers would stand out as people who forgave (Mt 6:14-15; 18:21-35) and were compassionate, generous, and unworldly (Lk 6:36-45).

This very brief summary shows that the teaching of Jesus makes radical demands on our way of living. It applies to each generation, and urgently to ours. Instead of accepting the level of behavior of his converts, Jesus demanded perfection. He said: "For if you love those who love you, what reward will you get? Do not even the tax collectors do as much? And if you save your greetings for your brothers, are you doing anything exceptional? Do not even the Gentiles do as much? You must therefore set no bounds to

your love, just as your heavenly Father sets none to his."
The phrase "set no bounds to your love" can also be
translated "be perfect."

This perfection illuminates all immorality, injustice, and
sin. We must go to war with sin, for sin enslaves us. Those
given to immorality are spiritually deaf and blind; they
cannot "hear" the one who preaches the gospel nor can they
"see" their condition and its destruction (Jn 8:34-38). Sin
makes us immune to grace, and therefore threatens our
salvation, for we are not saved *against our will.* God requires
our cooperation in our salvation. He *forces no one* to go to
Heaven!

GOD OR MONEY

Jesus said that it was impossible for a wealthy man to get
into the Kingdom of Heaven (Mt 19:23-26; Lk 18:24-27). In
fact, a camel would go through the eye of a needle more
quickly! Jesus spoke strongly against hoarding riches in
Luke 12:13-21. The man's soul was at stake, but he was only
concerned with his material wealth and the good life it
brought him. Jesus' judgment was that the man was a fool in
the real sense: he bartered his eternal salvation for material
things that he had to leave behind anyway. Such short-term
benefit for such long-term loss!

Some people think they can play the game both ways and
have both God and money. Such were the scribes and
Pharisees in Jesus' day. Many people today seek the
comforts of both money and religion, even preaching a
"prosperity gospel" while much of the world dies of
starvation.

Jesus was hard on this group—very hard! He warned that
his way was *not the way of the world.* It was the very opposite, a
very narrow way (Mt 7:13-14) involving self-denial. He
claimed that very few find this path of holiness. It is the way

of poverty, humility, heroic obedience to God's will, and service to humanity. Jesus said that the few who follow it are recognizable, for they stand out to the point of being persecuted for their faith and hated by the world (Jn 15:18-16:4). They are *like him* in showing the world its sinful ways and demanding repentance.

THE TRAP FOR RELIGIOUS PEOPLE

In Matthew 5:20 Jesus said that if our virtue went no deeper than that of the scribes and the Pharisees, we would never get into the Kingdom of Heaven. These people were very religious, but they fell into the trap of legalism, externalism, bigotry, piosity, and self-righteousness. They wanted power, prominence, popularity, and the first places in the synagogues. They were the experts to whom every-one turned for advice on religion. They were "gods" in the eyes of the people, who truly honored and obeyed them. Jesus said that they were in grave danger of Hell! (See Mt 6:5-6, 7-8; 15:1-20; 16:5-12; 23:1-36; Mk 12:38-40; Lk 11:37-54; 12:1-3; 13:22-30.)

The reason for Jesus' warning was that the attitudes of those who go to Heaven are humility, love, self-sacrifice, poverty, and service to others—attitudes diametrically opposed to those of the Pharisees. These religious people were very worldly, but it was cloaked in the guise of religion. Their behavior was no different from that of the unbelieving world, which operates on power politics, manipulation, and control of the many by the few. Jesus said that we are judged on our behavior; our social position means nothing to God.

IS EVERYONE SAVED?

The moral demands of Jesus were so challenging that he was asked one day, " 'Sir, will there be only a few saved?' He said to them, 'Try your hardest to enter by the narrow door, because, I tell you, many will try to enter and will not succeed' " (Lk 13:23-24). It will not be easy to get to Heaven. In fact, we have to apply a lot of energy to seeking God. Jesus went on to say to his immediate audience that there would be no point in telling him on the Day of Judgment that they knew his family or that he had preached on their streets (Lk 13:27). The rules are the same for everyone. Each person and nation is given time and grace to repent. If they don't cooperate with that grace, there will be consequences—the eternal loss of God's presence and the eternal loss of love. This is the ultimate frustration, described here as the "weeping and grinding of teeth."

TWENTY-ONE

Judgment in the Parables of Jesus

PARABLES REFLECT THE MIND OF JESUS. "He taught them in parables" is one of the clearest descriptions of his ministry. The themes of mercy and judgment run throughout this teaching.

FOUR RESPONSES

Let us take the parable of the sower (Mt 13:4-9, 18-23) as our first example. Here Jesus describes four responses to hearing the Word of God, and these responses represent the inner attitudes of his hearers. The first response is given by those who do not understand at all what is said. They are so worldly that the devil has no trouble removing the Word before it takes root. They are not listening, so how can they cooperate with God's Word? How can they do the will of God, which is essential to one who wants to go to Heaven?

The second group are those who receive the Word, even with delight (vs 20), but as soon as serving God begins to cost, they are off. They are *fair weather* Christians who are present when healings and miracles are handed out, but

205

refuse the cross. They want religion on their own terms, just as they want life their own way, so they do not persevere. They stand in contrast to the beatitude given to those who suffer for the Lord (Mt 5:11-12).

The third group are the most frightening, for they represent ordinary people who are just trying "to make ends meet." They listen to the Word, but it does not affect their lives, for they are taken up with "making their first million" or just the worries of everyday life. What goes on in church on Sunday has no bearing on the business of Monday to Saturday. And so the Word is choked.

None of these three groups produce any spiritual fruit, for they do not hear the Word of God and put it into practice. They are not true disciples of Jesus (Mk 3:35; Mt 7:21-27; Lk 6:46-49). Mercifully, there is a fourth group who hear the Word of God and do it. But they are in the minority, which underlines what Jesus said about the narrow way and the broad way in Matthew 7:13-14. The vast majority of people do not care about religion and the consequences for their eternal life, yet most of them believe that they will be saved!

STORIES OF THE JUDGMENT

In the parable of the darnel Jesus compares himself to a man who sows good seed in his field. An enemy comes and deliberately sows bad seed in order to spoil the crop. Jesus warns us that the devil is working to prevent our salvation. Because of his work there are good and bad in the church and in the world, called here the subjects of the Kingdom and subjects of the evil one (vss 38-39). How many people believe this today? Aren't we too sophisticated for this?

Jesus said that there will be a harvest time at the end of the world in which these groups will be separated. The harvest is one of his favorite images of the Final Judgment. It shows that history is proceeding towards a goal, a destiny. We are here for a purpose, and there will be a final summing up of events, with rewards and punishments meted out with real justice, regardless of the rank of the persons involved. Jesus himself is the Judge (vs 41), a right he has earned as our Paschal Lamb.

Revelation 6:16 says that in the final stages of the punishment of the nations, they will fear the wrath of the Lamb, for if the Savior becomes Judge there is no court of appeal. Here Jesus says that he will assign all who have persevered in evil to "the blazing furnace where there will be weeping and grinding of teeth." But the virtuous will shine like the sun in God's Kingdom. There are ultimate consequences of our behavior. The dragnet (Mt 13:47-50) is another parable that confirms this.

Jesus' story of the rich man and Lazarus, (Lk 16:19-31) is a warning to the rich concerning their treatment of their poor neighbors (see Mt 25:31-46). They will not be condemned for being rich, but for their neglect of charity, which is the greatest commandment of Jesus (Jn 13:13-17, 34). The poor man is not saved because he was poor, but because he trusted God to save him. He did not criticize or condemn the rich man, nor did he revile God for his condition.

The parable of the wedding feast (Mt 22:1-14; Lk 4:15-24), speaks about God's invitation to salvation, which is given to everyone. Jesus uses the image of a wedding feast to stress the joys of participation in God's Kingdom on earth, and also the joy and privilege of the elect in Heaven. Historically, the message of God's Kingdom was given to the Jews first, but by the time Jesus actually came, they were no longer interested (vs 5), for purely worldly reasons (vs 6). The punishment of the nation of Israel in the destruction of Jerusalem in A.D. 70 is the consequence (vs 7; see Lk 13:34-35; 19:41-44). This was followed by the proclamation of the Kingdom to all nations (vss 8-10). So the first stage of the parable shows that nations that reject the Word of God suffer consequences, and ultimately the loss of the Kingdom (see 21:33-43, esp vs 43).

The second half of the parable warns those who have come into the Kingdom that salvation is not automatic. Each must have his "wedding garment" on. Each must persevere in grace and in doing the will of God. At an oriental wedding feast the wedding garment was a gift from the host, so to refuse to wear it was an insult to the host that would not be missed by anyone present. In the same way, refusing salvation, which Jesus won for us on the cross and gave to us as a free gift, is an insult to God.

The guest without a wedding garment represents those who have heard the Christian call and received all the gifts of the Holy Spirit and all the grace necessary for salvation. They participate in the Eucharistic Banquet, which foreshadows the messianic banquet in Heaven. Nevertheless they are thrown out "into the darkness outside, where there will be weeping and grinding of teeth." This is a solemn warning to live a life worthy of the grace given.

WARNINGS FOR CHRISTIANS

The next set of parables deals with members of the church in the interim between the First and Second Comings of Jesus. In the parable of the conscientious steward (Mt 24:45-51), Jesus warns church leaders that they need to take care lest they abuse their position and fall into worldly immorality and injustice. Worldly leaders are in danger of being cut off and sent to Hell (vs 51) where they will be excluded from God's presence and love.

In Matthew 25:1-13 the bridesmaids represent the members of the church waiting for the Second Coming of Jesus, when he will begin the eternal messianic banquet. The parable uses the image of a Jewish wedding, where the women have to wait for the arrival of the groom and his attendants. Here the groom (Jesus) delays too long and some of them fall asleep, which is an image of spiritual inertia (see Mk 13:33-37). Only those disciples who have their faith burning with love—their lamps lit with oil—are ready when the Master returns. The others find themselves locked out of the feast, not because they were not invited but because they were slothful in spiritual matters.

The foolish virgins represent the "deathbed syndrome," the idea that people can convert at the last minute. They hope to make it into Heaven "by the skin of their teeth," having had the best of both worlds! They are deceiving themselves, and putting their eternal salvation in jeopardy. The parable says that those who did nothing about their spiritual lives were excluded from the feast.

In the parable of the talents (Mt 25:14-30; Lk 19:12-27), each servant has been gifted in some way by the Lord and is expected to use those gifts for the good of others. There will be a day of reckoning when we will be called to account for what we have done with the opportunities that have been given to us. Those who used their gifts will be rewarded, and those who remained inert spiritually will be punished. Their excuses are not accepted (vss 24-25), and they are given the maximum punishment: "As for this good-for-nothing servant, throw him into the darkness outside, where there will be weeping and grinding of teeth" (vs 30).

THE FINAL ACCOUNT

Matthew 25:31-45 gives the image of a king holding a day of reckoning with his servants. All must stand before him and before all the other servants to hear the judgment. No one knows initially why they are in two camps, one on the right and one on the left. But when the judgment is read, no one is left in doubt, and no one has any excuse. The judgment is based on love, and very practical love at that.

The Lord takes a dim view of those who take care of themselves to the neglect of everyone else (Lk 12:13-21; 16:19-31). The consequences of this neglect are too awful to think about, for "they will go away to eternal punishment" (vs 46). This is certainly not the way the world thinks! Psalm 49 shows the futility of the world's view, expressed simply as; "People praise you for looking after yourself" (vs 18). Jesus said that God's position is just the opposite, for he will praise you for taking care of your neighbors.

In this context we can understand the urgency of Jesus' words in Luke 9:25: "What benefit is it to anyone to win the whole world and forfeit or lose his very self?" Clearly Jesus' parables show that his Word is not a "take it or leave it" affair. There are eternal consequences for our actions. This is why he tells us to be radical about repentance (Mt 5:22, 26, 29-30).

After teaching and preaching to the lake towns of Galilee and working many miracles there, Jesus had hard words for those who refused to change their ways: "Alas for you, Chorazin! Alas for you, Bethsaida! for if the miracles done in you had been done in Tyre and Sidon, they would have repented long ago in sackcloth and ashes. Still, I tell you, that it will he more bearable for Tyre and Sidon on Judgment Day than for you. And as for you, Capernaum, did you want to be raised as high as heaven? You will be flung down to hell. For if the miracles done in you had been done in Sodom, it would be standing yet. Still, I tell you that it will be more bearable for Sodom on Judgment Day than for you" (Mt 11:20-24). God expects results for his work.

TWENTY-TWO

The Day of the Lord

B ELIEVERS OF BOTH the Old Testament and the New Testament view history as a series of interventions or visitations by God. The Lord was involved in the beginning as Creator, and since then as the Lord of history and controller of the universe. In fact, history is a continuous Advent of the Lord, and the cry of the believer is, "He came! He comes! He will come!" He came as Creator and Lord, he comes as Savior, and he will come as universal judge. No one escaped his visitations in the past, and no one will escape his visitations in the future. These visitations of God are called collectively "The Day of the Lord."

The Day of the Lord comes in one of two ways, either in Mercy or Judgment. Israel experienced both in the course of her history. God visited Israel in Egypt with mercy and salvation, but that same visitation meted out judgment to Egypt. Over a period of four hundred years Israel breached the Covenant and would not listen to the Word of God preached by the prophets. Then God visited the land with judgment in the Exile. Hence the Day of the Lord can be either one of joy or grief, depending on one's response to the Lord.

When Amos, for example, preached to the northern kingdom of Israel in the eighth century B.C., he declared that

211

the Day of the Lord would be one of judgment only. Corruption had spread through the land like a horrible disease, infecting priests and people alike. Yet the Israelites were so blind to their spiritual condition that they looked forward to the Lord's coming as if it were going to be a celebration (Am 5:18-20)! Amos's word was fulfilled with the destruction of Samaria and the mass deportation of the people to Assyria, where ten of the twelve tribes of Israel were lost forever.

The prophets of the eighth and seventh centuries B.C. taught that if the people persisted in sin, judgment would eventually overtake them (Is 1:21-26; 5:8-30; Am 3-6). Their final punishment was the destruction of Jerusalem and its glorious temple. What is said of Israel applies to all nations, for God is the Lord of history (see Am 1:3-2:16; Is 13-23; Jer 25:46-51).

THE LAST JUDGMENT

Originally the prophets thought that the Day of the Lord applied only to Israel (Ez 7-10), but gradually they began to think of it in universal terms (Is 24). All nations, as well as individuals, would have to give an account of their steward-ship before the King of Kings and Lord of Lords (Jl 4:12-14). For some it would be the time for rewards and for others a time for punishment, a combined day of joy and grief (Is 66:16; Wis 4:20-5:24). Only the sinners need fear this day, for the righteous are protected by God (Wis 3:1-12; 4:15).

The prophets used symbolic images to describe the Last Judgment. For Daniel, the end of the world (12:13) will be preceded by the "end times" (8:17-18; 11:35, 40; 12:4) which is a preparatory period. The great empires are "beasts" (Dn 7), who are stripped of their power when they appear before God in judgment. The one to whom all sovereignty, power, and glory are conferred is the mysterious Son of Man, the Supreme Judge, and his saints who rule with him (Dn 7:18, 22, 27).

Joel says that the sun and moon will grow dark, and the stars lose their brilliance, and the peoples of the earth will shake when the Lord roars from Zion (Jl 4:15-16). Isaiah says that the world will be judged by fire (Is 66:15-16).

Many of the psalms cry out to God to hasten this day, for it will bring true justice to the earth (Pss 75, 94, 96, 98, 140). Yet those who know God fear his judgment, for it is too just (Ps 143:2). They know that we are all sinners who are in desperate need of mercy. As the Gospels show very clearly, the only escape from this justice is to run to the Lord for mercy while there is still time.

THE DAY OF JESUS: HIS FIRST COMING

The Coming of Jesus in the Incarnation was the greatest divine visitation that the world has ever known. It was a visitation in mercy open to all without reserve. He is *the* prophet and the very *Word of God*. He revealed everything that God wanted us to know about himself, for he is *the truth* as well as the life and the way to God (Jn 14:6).

Jesus did not change the Old Testament concept of sin and judgment, and he did not deny that there was a Day of Judgment coming. He ratified these teachings, as we have illustrated from his parables. In fact, the Gospels show us that in Jesus, the eschatological judgment was already present, for everyone who came in contact with him had to take sides for or against him and his teachings, with eternal consequences.

John's Gospel speaks of the passage of Jesus through Israel as that of light through darkness (Jn 1:9-12; 3:19-21; 8:12; 9:5). This "x-ray light" showed up everything in the hearts of people, just as it exposed the spiritual condition of the nation. Jesus provided the light to anyone who wanted it (Jn 9), as he helped anyone willing to change (Jn 4) and cured their illnesses to prove God's love for them (Jn 5). Yet the light provoked rejection (9:40-41), and this meant that the judgment was already at work. The Last Judgment would be the final ratification of decisions made a long time previously. It is no different today, for the light of Christ shines in our world, and the Lord is passing by with his grace and salvation in this era of divine mercy. Our decisions have eternal consequences too.

Humanity's crime against God was the combined unbelief and consummate malice that brought about the condemnation and death of his beloved Son Jesus. This was humanity at war with God. Jesus commended himself to him who judges justly (1 Pt 2:21-25), and God's judgment was to raise him from the dead, an action that declared him innocent and humanity guilty (Jn 16:8-10). We can deal with our guilt by repenting (see Acts 2:37-41). But a world that continues with its unbelief, that persists in immorality and godlessness, can in no way avoid confrontation with God in the end (Rom 1-3).

Society today needs to hear the solemn warning of Psalm 50, for the final judgment will do no more than make manifest what is already at work in the world. "Everything now hidden will be made clear" (Mt 10:26-27). Amos, at the end of a long passage showing God's attempts to get through to his people says starkly, "Israel, prepare to meet your God!" (Am 4:12).

Jesus told the high priest at his trial, "Soon you will see the Son of Man seated at the right hand of the Power and coming on the clouds of heaven" (Mt 26:64). The One who stood before the high priest as the Paschal Lamb (Jn 1:29) in A.D. 30 would one day stand before him as his judge and the judge of all the nations (Rv 1:17; 5:5-8).

THE DAY OF JESUS: HIS SECOND COMING

The final judgment held a central place in the teaching of the early church (Acts 17:31; 24:25; 1 Pt 4:5). Unlike their Old Testament counterparts, they knew that the judge would be Jesus (Acts 2:36; 10:42; 17:31; Rom 2:16; 2 Tm 4:1). The judgment was seen as imminent (Jas 5:7-9), and all decisions were to be made in its light (1 Cor 4:5), for no one would escape it (Rom 2:4; Jude 15; Heb 9:27). They learned from God's previous dealings with Israel that when the time came, judgment would begin with the household of God (1 Pt 4:17-19).

Members of the church would be judged according to their works, no matter who they were or what were the circumstances of their lives (1 Pt 1:17; 1 Cor 3:11-15; Mt 16:27; 2 Cor 5, 10; Rv 20:12). Everything would be revealed then (Rom 2:16; 1 Cor 4:5) and tested by fire, even the heavens and the earth (2 Pt 3:7). Fornicators and adulterers would have a hard time on that day (Heb 13:4; Jas 4:4), as would anyone who sided with evil (2 Thes 2:12). Jesus would be the judge of the living and of the dead (2 Tm 4:1; Rv 19:11-16).

Those who had knowledge of God's Word in the Scriptures would be judged according to that (Jn 5:39-40, 45-47; Rom 2:12). Those who were deprived of God's Word would be judged according to the natural law written on their hearts (Rom 2:14-15). Christians would be judged by the standards of the gospel (Jas 2:10-13). Those who were especially privileged would be judged accordingly (Mt 11:22; Lk 12:48; Jn 15:22). Those who had judged others would be judged by their own standards (Rom 2:1; 14:10-12; Jas 2:13). Since no one is perfect, there is no room for complacency (Rom 3:10-20).

The apostolic teachers spoke of the Second Coming continuously, sometimes calling it an *apocalypsis,* which means a revelation of the Lord (2 Thes 1:7; 1 Pt 1:17, 13), or an *epiphaneia,* an appearing (1 Tm 6:14; Ti 2:13), or a *parousia,* a coming (Mt 24:3, 27; 1 Thes 2:19; 2 Thes 2:1). All of these terms speak of a definitive manifestation of Jesus as universal judge and Lord. They indicate an official visitation that no one can escape, a day that will truly be experienced as the Day of Christ.

All that was said in the Old Testament regarding the Last Judgment is now applied to Christ, the mysterious Son of Man whom Daniel spoke about. Both his origins and his destiny were with God, the Ancient of Days (Lk 17:24-30; Mt 16:27; 25:31; Mk 8:38; Lk 9:26). Jesus is the One who will come on the clouds of Heaven in power and great glory (Acts 1:11; Heb 9:28), in the presence of every living person (Mt 24:30; 26:64; Mk 13:26; 14:62; Lk 21:27), to manifest his triumph and to judge the living and the dead (Acts 10:42).

THE SHAKING OF THE NATIONS

The early church expected Jesus to return soon, initially within their own generation. Some people at Thessalonica had even given up work and were standing about waiting for Jesus to come. Paul's response was that Jesus should find them at their duties (2 Thes 3:10-15). He also described for them some clear signs of the Lord's return (2 Thes 2:1-12). Just as there had been a judgment for Israel at the beginning of the Christian era, so that era would end with the judgment of the nations of the earth (Lk 21:24). The judgment for Israel included the destruction of Jerusalem and its temple, and these are symbols of what awaits us at the end of time (Mt 24:1-3). There are proximate and long-term signs that will herald the Lord's coming, so we must learn to read the signs of the times we live in (Mt 16:1-4).

The initial signs of the end are false christs and false prophets who will deceive many. There will be wars, famines, and earthquakes, but this is just the beginning (Mt

24:4-8; Lk 21:8-10). Christians will be persecuted for their faith (Lk 21:12-17). Lawlessness will increase, and the love of many will grow cold (Mt 24:9-13). Meanwhile the gospel will be preached to the ends of the earth (Mt 24:14).

Paul speaks about a great revolt against God and a rebel who will exalt himself as though he were God (2 Thes 2:3-4). God holds him back until the appointed time, but the way is being prepared for him by the secret rebellion that is already at work in the world (2 Thes 2:7). Satan, the real enemy of God and the human race, needs this person to do his work for him. He will empower him with deceptive signs and miracles, and those who have not sought the truth through Jesus will succumb (2 Thes 2:9-12). This will lead to a decisive confrontation between the powers of good and evil in the earth (Rv 6-20). Jesus will overcome this rebel and all he stands for on the day of his appearing (2 Thes 2:8).

God will send many signs to the nations, just as he did to Israel in Amos's day (Am 4:1-12). Some of these signs will be in the form of punishments (Rv 6-11), in the hope of eliciting repentance from the nations. He will also raise up great witnesses to speak on his behalf (Rv 11; 12:17; 7:3-8).

Just as in the time of Noah, it will be a day of great sin and also a day of great grace (Mt 24:37-41). Very few will listen to God or follow his ways, just as happened then. God's judgment struck them unprepared, and only those who listened to God and to Noah were saved. Christians today have had plenty of time to listen to our Savior who so far surpasses anything that can be said of Noah (2 Thes 1:9). Luke 17:26-37 says that we need to learn the lessons of Lot and the cities of Sodom and Gomorrah also.

COME, LORD JESUS!

Jesus will return in the same way as he left in the Ascension (Acts 1:11), but we do not know the day nor the hour (1 Thes 5:2; Mt 24:27, 36; Lk 12:40; Rv 16:15). He will be preceded by cosmic signs; even the heavenly bodies will depart from their normal courses (Mt 24:29; Mk 13:34; Lk 21:25-27). Then the sign of the Son of Man will appear in the sky, and the Lord will gather his elect from the four corners of the globe (Mt 24:26-31). First the dead will be raised, then Jesus will call those who are still alive (1 Thes 4:13-17). Our Lord Jesus Christ will reveal himself to all nations (1 Cor 1:8), in the company of his saints (1 Thes 3:13).

The church awaits this moment with anticipation and joy, praying, "Maranatha, come Lord Jesus!" (Rv 22:17). This will be a wonderful day of salvation and the realization of her hope in the Lord (2 Tm 4:8; Ti 2:13). This *parousia* of Jesus is the consummation of history and the work of salvation, something to be desired by all who love him.

This belief that history reaches its climax in the judgment of the nations is basic to both the Old Testament and Christian faith. Our only choice with regard to this biblical teaching on sin and judgment is to throw out the Bible entirely or to prepare for the Day of Judgment. The ultimate choice is between divine mercy or divine judgment. The choice is ours; the consequences are eternal.

A final point for twentieth-century Christians. If we consider the biblical reckoning of time that with the Lord a thousand years is like a single day (Ps 90:4; 2 Pt 3:8), we are about to enter the third day since the Resurrection! Since Christ rose from the dead on the third day, might he not also return in the *parousia* on the third day? It is really true that Jesus is coming soon (Phil 4:5; Heb 10:37; Jas 5:8; Rv 3:11; 22:20)!

We Meet Jesus:
The Word in the Word of God

THERE ARE TWO PIECES OF ADVICE for anyone who has persevered this far. One, I consider it an absolute necessity to read and pray the Word of God daily. There alone we meet with the "it" and the "him" of God's Word and know its transforming power for us personally. Only when we confront the mystery of the Word will we understand Hebrews 4:12: "The Word of God is something alive and active: it cuts more incisively than any two-edged sword; it can seek out the place where soul is divided from the spirit, or joints from marrow; it can pass judgment on secret emotions and thoughts. No created thing is hidden from him; everything is uncovered and stretched fully open to the eyes of the one to whom we must give an account of ourselves."

Here is a little secret of success for uncovering the mystery of the Word: the child of God (that's me) takes the Word of God (the Scriptures) into the presence of God (prayer) and lets the Holy Spirit of God (the Author) make that Word come to life for me and, more importantly, in me. The extraordinary thing about the Scriptures is that even if you take a passage that you do not technically understand (in the scholarly sense), that in no way blocks the Lord from explaining it to you or from giving you the grace it speaks about. He does not leave you short-changed because you lack technical knowledge. As we have seen, his judgment is based not on knowledge but on love. All of us can grow to perfection in that. We can become like him whom we cannot explain intellectually, but whom we can know very personally through faith and love.

A second bit of advice: if you want to prove to yourself or anyone else that Scripture is the Word of God, then I suggest that you put the teaching of Jesus on forgiveness into practice. You will see for yourself the freedom it brings into your life and your relationships. If you wish to become an untechnical expert (a new phenomenon!), then take the passage of Mark 1:40-45 on the healing of the leper, and pray it for one hour each day for the weeks or months that are required to crack open its mystery. Then I will be happy to read *your* book on the good news of Jesus Christ, for this little scene all by itself is a summary of the gospel.

You need to place yourself at the foot of the cross beside Mary of Magdala and ask her to explain her deliverance from the leprosy of evil and the sheer glory of being Jesus' disciple. Speak to the Queen of Martyrs on the price her Son had to pay for this freedom. If you have the courage, look up and see Jesus, dying as a leper on the cross, not with the physical disease of leprosy but with the sins of all of us. He is *the martyr* and the model of all other martyrs. He is *the victim* and the model of all other innocent victims of violence. Then perhaps you will begin to realize anew just what love is— divine love, forgiving love, healing love, transforming love— and you will understand Mary of Magdala's adoration despite the scorn and insults of everybody around her.

Then speak to the Apostle John, who wrote the most spiritual Gospel, having clung to Jesus during his lifetime and remaining faithful to the end. He was close to Jesus and Mary, for he took care of the mother after the Son's death. Read what he proclaimed to the world after his experience of divine love from Jesus and extraordinary sanctity from

Mary. Tradition tells us that he literally never stopped talking about love—God's love (1 Jn 4) and the love we need to return to him. He was the beloved disciple who drank God's pure love straight from the heart of Jesus both in life and in death, so he can enlighten you.

Try, if you can, to kneel beside Mary of Magdala. Look up at Jesus and say to him "I am your leper." But only say it when you are ready for what will happen, for the floodgates of grace will open to you, and then there will be two "Mary of Magdala's" there, and you will never be the same. Your adoration of Jesus the Savior will never exhaust itself; it will renew itself with each outpouring of love and service, adoration and praise, even here in this life. And you will be given the certainty deep within your being that the leprosy is gone forever. You are no longer the old sinner but the new disciple, loved and lovely.

There are other things to be experienced here at the foot of the cross, the center of all life, but you must find them for yourself. When you experience the Word like this, you are left in no doubt that "this is the Word of God!"

You also learn something that the books cannot teach you; only another disciple can pass it on. It is that the Scriptures in your hands, in prayer, have the selfsame power to heal, change, challenge, and transform lives as they had when Jesus spoke. They have not lost their power nor the presence of him who breathed upon the human authors. Jesus is alive today, in his church and in you. As you open the book, open your heart in prayer, for he is speaking and giving grace just as he did in Capernaum, the place that is still called "the town of Jesus."

Old Testament Prophecies Find Their Fulfillment in Jesus

WE HAVE BEEN TOLD THAT the life of Jesus of Nazareth was a fulfillment of the Scriptures, that the Old Testament prophecies had spoken about him, yet few of us have the opportunity to look up the evidence for ourselves. I have included here a list of Old Testament texts taken from the Thompson Chain-reference Bible to try to make an attempt at such an illustration. A list like this cannot be absolutely exact. It attempts to show that you can find various events in the life of Christ referred to in the Old Testament texts.

Begin by reading the headings: Jesus was to be of the offspring of woman, also of Abraham and the patriarchs, the Fathers of the Chosen People. He was to be from the tribe of Judah, and the heir to the throne of David. The place and time of his birth are given, and that he was to be born of a virgin ... and so on.

Having read the headings then proceed to look at the left hand side column where the relevant Old Testament text is given and then on the right hand side at its New Testament counterpart. These are illustrations not proofs, just to show you that the Old Testament does indeed refer to Jesus everywhere, but not by name. He is referred to by his function as Messiah, Savior, the Promised One, or the Man of Sorrows, etc. It is by looking at these texts through the New Testament that we see more clearly what must have been vague for those before Christ.

PROPHECIES	FULLFILLMENT

Would be the "Offspring of a Woman"

Gn 3:15 And I will put enmity between you and the woman, and between your offspring and hers; he will crush his head, and you will strike his heel.

Gal 4:4 But when the time had fully come, God sent his Son, born of a woman, born under law. (Lk 2:7; Rv 12:5)

Promised Offspring of Abraham

Gn 18:18 Abraham will surely become a great and powerful nation, and all nations on earth will be blessed through him. (Gn 12:3)

Acts 3:25 And you are heirs of the prophets and of the covenant God made with your fathers. He said to Abraham, "Through your offspring all peoples on earth will be blessed." (Mt 1:1; Lk 3:34)

Promised Offspring of Isaac

Gn 17:19 Then God said, "Yes, but your wife Sarah will bear you a son, and you will call him Isaac. I will establish my covenant with him as an everlasting covenant for his descendants after him."

Mt 1:2 Abraham was the father of Isaac, Isaac the father of Jacob, Jacob the father of Judah and his brothers. (Lk 3:34)

Promised Offspring of Jacob

Nm 24:17 I see him, but not now; I behold him, but not near. A star will come out of Jacob; a scepter will rise out of Israel. He will crush the foreheads of Moab, the skulls of all the sons of Sheth. (Gn 28:14)

Lk 3:34 The son of Jacob, the son of Isaac, the son of Abraham, the son of Terah, the son of Nahor. (Mt 1:2)

PROPHECIES	FULFILLMENT

Will descend from the tribe of Judah

Gn 49:10 The scepter will not depart from Judah, nor the ruler's staff from between his feet, until he comes to whom it belongs and the obedience of the nations is his.	**Lk 3:33** The son of Amminadab, the son of Ram, the son of Hezron, the son of Perez, the son of Judah. (Mt 1:2-3)

The heir to the throne of David

Is 9:7 Of the increase of his government and peace there will be no end. He will reign on David's throne and over his kingdom, establishing and upholding it with justice and righteousness from that time on and forever. The zeal of the Lord Almighty will accomplish this. (Is 11:1-5; 2 Sm 7:13)	**Mt 1:1** A record of the genealogy of Jesus Christ the son of David, the son of Abraham. (Mt 1:6)

Place of birth

Mi 5:2 But you, Bethlehem Ephrathah, though you are small among the clans of Judah, out of you will come for me one who will be ruler over Israel, whose origins are from of old, from ancient times.	**Mt 2:1** After Jesus was born in Bethlehem in Judea, during the time of King Herod, Magi from the east came to Jerusalem. (Lk 2:4-7)

PROPHECIES	FULFILLMENT

Time of birth

Dn 9:25 Know and understand this: From the issuing of the decree to restore and rebuild Jerusalem until the Anointed One, the ruler, comes, there will be seven "sevens," and sixty-two "sevens."	**Lk 2:1-2** In those days Caesar Augustus issued a decree that a census should be taken of the entire Roman world. [This was the first census that took place while Quirinius was governor of Syria.] (Lk 2:3-7)

Born of a virgin

Is 7:14 Therefore the Lord himself will give you a sign. The virgin will be with child and will give birth to a son, and will call him Immanuel.	**Mt 1:18** This is how the birth of Jesus Christ came about. His mother Mary was pledged to be married to Joseph, but before they came together, she was found to be with child through the Holy Spirit. (Lk 1:26-35)

Slaughter of infants

Jer 31:15 This is what the Lord says, "A voice is heard in Ramah mourning and great weeping. Rachel weeping for her children and refusing to be comforted, because her children are no more."	**Mt 2:16** When Herod realized that he had been outwitted by the Magi, he was furious, and he gave orders to kill all the boys in Bethlehem and its vicinity who were two years old and under, in accordance with the time he had learned from the Magi. (Mt 2:17-18)

PROPHECIES	FULFILLMENT

Escape into Egypt

Hos 11:1 When Israel was a child, I loved him, and out of Egypt I called my son.

Mt 2:14 So he got up, took the child and his mother during the night, and left for Egypt.

Ministry in Galilee

Is 8:1-2 Nevertheless, there will be no more gloom for those who were in distress. In the past he humbled the land of Zebulun and the land of Naphtali, but in the future he will honor Galilee of the Gentiles, by the way of the sea, along the Jordan. The people walking in darkness have seen a great light; on those living in the land of the shadow of death a light has dawned.

Mt 4:12-16 When Jesus heard that John had been put in prison, he returned to Galilee. Leaving Nazareth, he went and lived in Capernaum, which was by the lake in the area of Zebulun and Naphtali—to fulfill what was said through the prophet Isaiah: "Land of Zebulun and land of Naphtali, the way to the sea, along the Jordan. Galilee of the Gentiles—the people living in darkness have seen a great light; on those living in the land of the shadow of death a light has dawned."

As a prophet

Dt 18:15 The Lord your God will raise up for you a prophet like me from among your own brothers. You must listen to him.

Jn 6:14 After the people saw the miraculous sign that Jesus did, they began to say, "Surely this is the Prophet who is to come into the world." (Jn 1:45; Acts 3:19-26)

PROPHECIES	FULFILLMENT

As a priest, like Melchizedek

Ps 110:4 The Lord has sworn and will not change his mind: "You are a priest forever, in the order of Melchizedek."	**Heb 6:20** Jesus, who went before us, has entered on our behalf. He had become a high priest forever, in the order of Melchizedek. (Heb 5:5-6; 7:15-17)

He was rejected by Jews

Is 53:3 He was despised and rejected by men, a man of sorrows, and familiar with suffering. Like one from whom men hide their faces he was despised, and we esteemed him not. (Ps 2:2)	**Jn 1:11** He came to that which was his own, but his own did not receive him. (Jn 5:43; Lk 4:29; 17:25; 23:18)

Some of his characteristics

Is 11:2 The Spirit of the Lord will rest on him—the Spirit of wisdom and of under-standing, the Spirit of counsel and of power, the Spirit of knowledge and of the fear of the Lord. (Ps 45:7; Is 11:3-4)	**Lk 2:52** And Jesus grew in wisdom and stature, and in favor with God and men. (Lk 4:18)

Jesus' triumphal entry into Jerusalem

Zec 9:9 Rejoice greatly, O Daughter of Zion! Shout, Daughter of Jerusalem! See, your king comes to you, righteous and having salvation, gentle and riding on a donkey, on a colt, the foal of a donkey. (Is 62:11)	**Jn 12:13-14** They took palm branches and went out to meet him, shouting, "Ho-sanna!" "Blessed is he who comes in the name of the Lord!" "Blessed is the King of Israel!" Jesus found a young donkey and sat upon it, as it is written. (Mt 21:1-11; Jn 12:12)

PROPHECIES	FULFILLMENT

Betrayed by a friend

Ps 41:9 Even my close friend, whom I trusted, he who shared my bread, has lifted up his heel against me.

Mk 14:10 Then Judas Iscariot, one of the Twelve, went to the chief priests to betray Jesus to them. (Mt 26:14-16; Mk 14:43-45)

Sold for thirty pieces of silver

Zec 11:12 I told them, "If you think it best, give me my pay; but if not, keep it." So they paid me thirty pieces of silver. (Zec 11:13)

Mt 26:15 [Judas] asked, "What are you willing to give me if I hand him over to you?" So they counted out for him thirty silver coins. (Mt 27:3-10)

Money returned for a potter's field

Zec 11:13 And the Lord said to me, "Throw it to the potter"—the handsome price at which they priced me! So I took the thirty pieces of silver and threw them into the house of the Lord to the potter.

Mt 27:5-7 Judas flung the money into the temple and left . . . The chief priests picked up the coins and said, "It is against the law to put this into the treasury, since it is blood money." So they decided to use the money to buy the potter's field as a burial place for foreigners. (Mt 27:3-5; 8-10)

PROPHECIES	FULFILLMENT

Judas's position to be taken by another

Ps 109:7-8 When he is tried, let him be found guilty, and may his prayers condemn him. May his days be few; may another take his place of leadership.	**Acts 1:18-20** (With the reward he got for his wickedness, Judas bought a field; there he fell headlong, his body burst open and all his intestines spilled out. Everyone in Jerusalem heard about this, so they called that field in their language Akeldama, tha is, Field of Blood.) "For," said Peter, "it is written in the book of Psalms, 'May his place be deserted; let there be no one to dwell in it,' and , 'May another take his place of leadership.' "(Acts 1:16-17)

False witnesses accuse Jesus

Ps 27:12 Do not turn me over to the desire of my foes, for false witnesses rise up against me, breathing out violence. (Ps 35:11)	**Mt 26:60-61** Many false witnesses came forward. Finally two came forward and declared, "This fellow said, 'I am able to destroy the temple of God and rebuild it in three days.' "

PROPHECIES	FULFILLMENT

Silent when accused

Is 53:7 He was oppressed and afflicted, yet he did not open his mouth; he was led like a lamb to the slaughter, and as a sheep before her shearers is silent, so he did not open his mouth. (Ps 38:13-14)

Mt 26:62-63 Then the high priest stood up and said to Jesus, "Are you not going to answer? What is this testimony that these men are bringing against you?" But Jesus remained silent. The high priest said to him, "I charge you under oath by the living God: Tell us if you are the Christ, the Son of God." (Mt 27:12-14)

Struck and spit on

Is 5:6 I offered my back to those who beat me, my cheeks to those who pulled out my beard. I did not hide my face from mocking and spitting.

Mk 14:65 Then some began to spit at him; they blindfolded him, struck him with their fists, and said, "Prophesy!" and the guards took him and beat him. (Mk 15:17; Jn 19:1-3; 18:22)

Hated without cause

Ps 69:4 Those who hate me without reason outnumber the hairs of my head; many are my enemies without cause, those who seek to destroy me. I am forced to restore what I did not steal. (Ps 109:3-5)

Jn 15:23-25 He who hates me hates my Father as well. If I had not done among them what no one else did, they would not be guilty of sin. But now they have seen these miracles, and yet they have hated both me and my Father. But this is to fulfill what is written in their law, "They hated me without reason."

PROPHECIES	FULFILLMENT

Suffered vicariously

Is 53:4-5 Surely he took up our infirmities and carried our sorrows, yet we considered him stricken by God, smitten by him, and afflicted. But he was pierced for our transgressions, he was crushed for our iniquities; the punishment that brought us peace was upon him, and by his wounds we are healed. (Is 53:6, 12)

Mt 8:16-17 When evening came, many who were demon-possessed were brought to him, and he drove out the spirits with a word and healed all the sick. This was to fulfill what was spoken through the prophet Isaiah: "He took up our infirmities and carried our diseases." (Rom 4:25; 1 Cor 15:3)

Crucified with sinners

Is 53:12 He poured out his life unto death, and was numbered with the transgressors. For he bore the sin of many, and made intercession for the transgressors.

Mt 27:38 Two robbers were crucified with him, one on his right and one on his left. (Mk 15:27-28; Lk 23:33)

Hands and feet pierced

Ps 22:16 Dogs have surrounded me; a band of evil men has encircled me, they have pierced my hands and my feet. (Zec 12:10)

Jn 20:27 Then he said to Thomas, "Put your finger here, see my hands. Reach out your hand and put it into my side. Stop doubting and believe." (Jn 19:37; 20:25-26)

PROPHECIES	FULFILLMENT

Mocked and Insulted

Ps 22:6-8 But I am a worm and not a man, scorned by men and despised by the people. All who see me mock me; they hurl insults, shaking their heads and saying, "He trusts in the Lord; let the Lord rescue him. Let him deliver him, since he delights in him."	**Mt 27:39-40** Those who passed by hurled insults at him, shaking their heads and saying, "You who were going to destroy the temple and build it in three days, save yourself! Come down from the cross, if you are the Son of God!" (Mt 27:41-44; Mk 15:29-32)

Given gall and vinegar

Ps 69:21 They put gall in my food and gave me vinegar for my thirst.	**Jn 19:29** A jar of wine vinegar was there, so they soaked a sponge in it, put the sponge on a stalk of the hyssop plant, and lifted it to Jesus' lips. (Mt 27:34, 48)

Hears prophetic words repeated in mockery

Ps 22:8 He trusts in the Lord; let the Lord rescue him. Let him deliver him, since he delights in him.	**Mt 27:41, 43** The chief priests, the scribes, and the elders also joined in the jeering: . . . "He trusts in God. Let God rescue him now if he wants him, for he said, 'I am the Son of God.' "

Prays for his enemies

Ps 109:4 In return for my friendship they accuse me, but I am a man of prayer. (Is 53:12)	**Lk 23:34** Jesus said, "Father, forgive them, for they do not know what they are doing."

PROPHECIES	FULFILLMENT

His side to be pierced

Zec 12:10 And I will pour out on the house of David and the inhabitants of Jerusalem a spirit of grace and supplication. They will look on me, the one they have pierced, and they will mourn for him as one mourns for an only child, and grieve bitterly for him as one grieves for a firstborn son.	**Jn 19:34** One of the soldiers pierced Jesus' side with a spear, bringing a sudden flow of blood and water.

Soldiers cast lots for his clothes

Ps 22:18 They divide my garments among them and cast lots for my clothing.	**Mk 15:24** And they crucified him. Dividing up his clothes, they cast lots to see what each would get. (Jn 19:24)

Not a bone to be broken

Ps 34:20 He protects all his bones, not one of them will be broken. (Ex 12:46)	**Jn 19:33** But when they came to Jesus and found that he was already dead, they did not break his legs.

PROPHECIES	FULFILLMENT

To be buried with the rich

Is 53:9 He was assigned a grave with the wicked, and with the rich in his death, though he had done no violence, nor was any deceit in his mouth.	**Mt 27:57-60** As evening approached, there came a rich man from Arimathea, named Joseph, who had himself become a disciple of Jesus. Going to Pilate, he asked for Jesus' body, and Pilate ordered that it be given to him. Joseph took the body, wrapped it in a clean linen cloth, and placed it in his own new tomb that he had cut out of the rock. He rolled a big stone in front of the entrance to the tomb and went away.

His Resurrection

Ps 16:10 Because you will not abandon me to the grave, nor will you let your Holy One see decay. (Mt 16:21)	**Mt 28:9** Suddenly Jesus met them. "Greetings," he said. They came to him, clasped his feet, and worshiped him. (Lk 24:36-48)

His ascension

Ps 68:18 When you ascended on high, you led captives in your train; you received gifts from men, even from the rebellious—that you, O Lord God, might dwell there.	**Lk 24:50-51** When he had led them out to the vicinity of Bethany, he lifted up his hands and blessed them. While he was blessing them, he left them and was taken up into heaven. (Acts 1:9)

Other Books of Interest
from Servant Publications

You Can Understand the Old Testament
A Book-by-Book Guide for Catholics
Peter Kreeft

For many lay Catholics, reading and studying the Old Testament is intimidating and overwhelming. For starters, there are so many books and several different types of books—from history to prophecy, from poetry to philosophy. Where do you start reading? And how can you even begin to understand what you're reading—given the scholarly issues of authorship, history, archaeology, and the meaning of the original Hebrew and Greek?

Now Peter Kreeft, in *You Can Understand the Old Testament*, offers the reader a clear road map. With keen insight and engaging wit, Kreeft focuses on the core message of each book and its relevance for today, making for both enjoyable and spiritually satisfying reading. For Catholics who thought they could never enjoy the Old Testament, it's time to take another look. *$8.95*

Catholic Questions, Catholic Answers
Father Kenneth Ryan

- Is there really a place called Purgatory?
- Who wrote the Bible?
- What will happen at the end of the world?

These and dozens of other provocative questions are answered in the inimitable style of Father Kenneth Ryan.

Within these pages, nearly every aspect of Catholic life is covered, including questions on the saints, Mary, church doctrine, devotions, the Bible, the pope, the liturgy, and even the real beliefs and evangelistic tactics of cults like the Jehovah's Witnesses. *Catholic Questions, Catholic Answers* is a fascinating, inspiring, and informative treasury of facts and truths about the church. *$7.95*